America in Focus

Life, Liberty and the Pursuit of Happiness

Those Inalienable Rights

by
Erwin Helms

Teacher's Book

Ferdinand Schöningh 41152 7

Unterrichtsmaterialien für die Sekundarstufe II

America in Focus
Britain in Focus

herausgegeben von Dr. Peter H. Stoldt

Life, Liberty and the Pursuit of Happiness

Those Inalienable Rights

Texte zusammengestellt und bearbeitet von:

Dr. Erwin Helms und Henry Cooke

(Verlag Ferdinand Schöningh, Jühenplatz 1, D 4790 Paderborn)

Printed in Germany. Gesamtherstellung Ferdinand Schöningh.

Druck 5 4 3 2

ISBN 3-506-41152-7

Contents

Preface 5
The Objectives of the Course 6
How to Get the Course Started 8
▪Additional Text: John Stuart Mill "On Liberty" 9

Introduction (Texts 1-4) 12
Introductory Comments 12
•Special Feature: Note-taking 12
Text 1: The Declaration of Independence, 1776 13
•Additional Text: H.D. Thoreau, "Civil Disobedience" 13
•Special Feature: The Organization and Delivery of Speeches 15
Text 2:First Ten Amendments to the U.S. Constitution 16
▪Additional Text: F.D. Roosevelt: "The Four Freedoms" 18
Text 4: Samuel F. Smith: "America", 1832 18

Church and State (Texts 5-14) 19
Introductory Comments 19
Text 5: The Scopes Trial, 1925 20
▪Additional Text: The American Civil Liberties Union 20
Text 6: West Virginia Board of Education v. Barnette, 1943 23
▪Additional Text: The Star-Spangled Banner 24
Text 7: A Legal Battle 25
Text 8: Newsweek Report on the Lord's Prayer Decision, 1963 25
▪Additional Text: Everson v. The Board of Education, Ewing, NJ, 1947 26
Text 9: The Jesus Mania 28
Text 10: Macho Christianity: The Success of Jerry Falwell 29
•Special Feature: Debating and Discussing 31
Church Advertisements (Text 10) 34
Text 11: American Coalition of Traditional Values (ACTV) 34
Text 12: Ten Basis Concerns of the Evangelical Christian Community 34
▪Additional Text: Teenagers in Trouble 36
Text 13: Christian Voice: Report Card 40
Text 14: The Bishops Call a "Halt" 41

Gender and the Constitution (Texts 15-23) 42
Introductory Comments 42
Text 15: Alexis de Tocqueville: Democracy in America 42
Text 16: The Seneca Falls Declaration, 1848 43
Text 18: Tennessee Williams: The Glass Menagerie 43
Text 19: Sylvia Plath: Too Many Choices 44
▪Additional Text: Excerpts from Sylvia Plath's Journals 45
Text 20: Betty Friedan: The Crisis in Women's Identity 47
Text 21: The National Organisation of Women's Statement of Purpose, 1966 47
▪Additional Text: Data: Women in Employment 47
▪Additional Text: Women's Liberation: A Black Perspective 50
Text 22: The Proposed Equal Rights Amendment 52
▪Additional Text: The Equal Rights Amendment: No 53
Interview with Mrs Phyllis Schafly 56
Text 23: A Humorous Commentary on the Feminist Movement 56

The Constitution and the Black People (Texts 24-31) 57
Introductory Comments 57
Text 24: The Emancipation Proclamation, 1863 57
Text 25: The 13th, 14th, 15th Amendments (1865-1870) 58

Text 26: The Civil Rights Act of 1875 58
Additional Text: One Negro who's not going to vote 59
Text 27: Intimidation of the Black Population 59
Leaflet of the Ku Klux Klan 59
▪Additional Text: Leaflet of the White Citizens'Council 60
Claude Mc Kay: The Lynching 61
Text 28: Brown v. Broad of Education of Topeca, 1954 62
▪Additional Text: Data on Blacks 62
Text 29: Eldridge Cleaver: Soul on Ice 64
▪Additional Text: Why I left the U.S. and Why I am returning 65
▪Additional Text: "How the Prophet of Violence became the Apostle of Brotherhood" 65
Text 30: Program of the Black Panther Party 66
Text 31: The Allan Bakke Case 70
▪Additional Text: Jesse Jackson "Our Time Has Come" 71

The Constitution and Other Individual Rights (Text 32-40)
Introductory Comments 73
A "The right to bear arms 73
Text 32: "If Guns Were Outlawed, Only Outlaws Would Have Guns" 74
Text 33: The Subway Gunman 75
Text 34: The Dangers of Self-Defense 75
▪Additional Text: A Newsweek Poll "Deadly Force" 75
▪Additional Text: George F. Will "Let Us Now Praise" 77
B Freedom of Speech and of the Press 78
Additional Text: Freedom of Information Act 79
Text 37: Near v. Minnesota 81
Text 38: Ellsberg and the Pentagon Papers 82
Text 39: U.S. Government v. New York Times and Washington Post, 1971 83
Text 40: The Watergate Scandal 83
▪Additional Text: Walter Lippmann: Debate As The Essential Principle of Freedom of Speech 84
Additional Topic: The Fourth Amendment: Search and Seizure 85

Basic Principles (Texts 41-44)
Federalism - Checks and Balances - Grassroots Democracy 89
A Federalism 89
Text 41: Ronald Reagan: "New Federalism" State of the Union Message, Jan. 20, 1982 90
▪Additional text: Edward M. Kennedy: Federalism and the Progressive Vision 91
B Separation of Powers and Checks and Balances (Texts 42-43) 93
▪Additional Text: Examples of How the Constitution Divides Powers 95
C Grassroots Democracy (Texts 44-45) 96
Text 44: The Port Huron Statements, 1962 96
Additional Text: George F. Kennan "Rebels without a Program" 97
Conclusion 101
Text 45: Teenagers View the Constitution 101
▪Additional Text: "Intent of the Framers", Newsweek 101
Summary 103
Selected Bibliography 104
List of Resource Centers 110
Appendix 112
The Declaration of Independence 113
The Constitution of the United States 117
Grundgesetz für die Bundesrepublik Deutschland 135
Universal Declaration of Human Rights 140

PREFACE

Since Leslie C. High, Chief of the American Studies Branch Of the United States Information Service, suggested to me at a visit to his office in Washington D.C. that I might prepare a documentation on the US Constitution on the occasion of its 200th anniversary, I have been working on this project. To my delight, the Schöningh publishing house gave the project its full support from the beginning and helped immensely to get the Students'and Teacher's Books ready for the bicentennial.

I am grateful to Henry Cooke Jr. for his excellent contributions to the Students' Book, to Mrs. L. Tiedje and Mrs. U. Truman, the librarians of the Amerikahaus Hannover, for providing me with bibliographical information and data, to Dr. Brian Tracy, until recently Director of the Deutsch-Amerika-Institut in Heidelberg, for going through the final version of the Teacher's Book and to Dr. Peter H. Stoldt, the editor of this series, and to the Schöningh publishing house, esp. to Gerald T. Williams, for their encouragement, critism and advice.

The Objectives of the Course

In 1987 the Americans celebrated the bicentennial of their Constitution. This event is of interest not only to the Americans; other countries, among them the Federal Republic of Germany, and various international organizations have adopted constitutions or charters that are based on the model of the American Constitution. It also raises more fundamental questions:
What explains the fact that a constitution written at the end of the 18th century has lasted so long? By what procedures has it been kept flexible enough to adapt to changing conditions?
In an attempt to answer these questions it should be kept in mind, as was also pointed out in the Students'Book, that when the Founding Fathers devised the Constitution, the U.S.A. was made up of only thirteen states and its population chiefly rural and predominantly of British stock.
How was a Constitution based on these premises able to stand the test of time, and meet the requirements of a nation which in the following 200 years changed into an industrialized, highly urbanized, and multi-ethnic society?

This collection of non-fictional and fictional texts will, by drawing on issues of the past and the present which have appeared and are appearing in similar form in other countries, attempt to analyse the fundamental principles on which the Constitution is based.
As it is impossible to discuss all aspects of the Constitution and as a mere "Institutionskunde" would not motivate our students, case studies of how particular issues were and are resolved within the political system and how the life of American citizens was affected, will be presented, i.e.

the relationship between church and state,
the issue of gender,
the black people's fight for freedom and equality,
the right to bear arms and its consequences, and
the freedom of speech and of the press.

The analyses of these case studies will enable the students to understand such basic principles as

federalism,
government by checks and balances,
and government based on the consent of the governed.

As the cases presented and the principles discussed are often interrelated, the material in this collection may be used in various combinations. At the beginning of the course, teacher and students should get together to decide in what order the topics are to be dealt with.
This book will furnish the teacher with supplementary exercises (printed in italics) and with additional material (marked ■) which may be used for tests or reports by individuals or groups of students, and also with advice on where other pertinent texts and surveys may be found, so that you may deal with a topic in greater depth (see bibliography and addresses of Resource Centers pp. 101-110). Students should also be encouraged to look for reports on current events which are related to various aspects presented in the Students' book.
As the students will be expected to check the universal validity of the basic principles, it is recommended they seek comparison with other subjects, such as History, "Gemeinschaftskunde" and Geography. Such a procedure is especially advisable when the US Constitution is compared with the "Grundgesetz", the Charter of the United Nations and of the European Community (see Appendix).

To sum up:

1. This course is meant to give the students an insight into the role of the Constitution within the political system,
2. to inform them about the major constitutional principles and their application,
3. to make the students understand formal and informal changes in the Constitution, and
4. to show them how the Constitution works, what the government may do for its citizens, and what the citizens can do to sustain civil liberties.

This procedure will show the students how the Americans cope with political and social problems using the instrument of the Constitution. It will also familiarize them with historical events that shaped America and with values the Americans cherish.
As the rather legalistic language of the Constitution might possibly scare the students away, quotations from it are kept to a minimum. For your own information its full text is reprinted as in the Appendix, so you might introduce passages from it when you consider it necessary.
The need for student inquiry and investigation is fundamental to his course of study. The intention is to teach them "how to learn". Some of the questions posed in the Students'Book do not have one correct answer only, but the search for an answer will lead to the development of critical thinking.

To achieve this goal, both facts **and** opinions, often controversial, are offered, thus making the students realize the difference between facts and comments. C. P. Scott's (1846 - 1932), the famous editor of the Manchester Guardian, dictum "Comment is free but facts are sacred" should be a guiding principle throughout.
The texts - documents, speeches, interviews, court decisions, magazine articles, leaflets, diagrams, statistics, cartoons, and illustrations as well as essays, poems and selections from fictional literature - will give the students practice in analysing non-fictional and fictional material.
A central concern is, of course, the improvement of the language skills of the students:

- their oral competence
- their reading and writing skills
- their insight into language registers (formal, informal, slang, dialect) and into the main differences between British and American English(1), and
- their skill in group interaction (dialogue participation, concentration on the topic under discussion, adjustment to criticism etc.)

The questions and exercises in the Student's Book are suggestions. Before they are dealt with, the students should be encouraged to make their own comments and pose their own questions.
It is frequently much more likely that a lively discussion will ensue, when the students are left to themselves. The teacher's main function at this stage is to see to it that the students stick to the topic.

Some special features marked ● (note-taking, organization and delivery of speeches, debating and discussion) outline exercises that may be used throughout the course.

(1) All texts taken from American sources have American spelling.

How to Get the Course Started

In order to motivate the students for the topic, they can be made aware that they are surrounded in their everyday life by statutes and regulations. On their way to school they have to look out for traffic lights, obey signs and speed limits.
If they are members of a club or play games, they follow rules. If a member of the opposing team does not play fair, they are likely to cry 'foul'. Often they follow and accept these rules more or less unconsciously.
To make them aware of the need for rules and regulations in human relationships, they could be asked how they would proceed if they were to found a club of their own. Ask them to name what they need for such a project. Write down their suggestions on the blackboard as they come, then discuss them and ultimately have the students arrange them in a logical order. This may in the end result in a list similar to the following. (A)
If you then transfer this list to a nation, you will get a scheme which reveals that nations arrange their political systems in a very similar fashion. (B)

A. Club		B. Nation
must outline its goals	PREAMBLE	fix its raison d'être
must appoint officers who act in its name fix their functions	EXECUTIVE	outline who is to represent the people, how is he/she to be elected, what are his/her functions who will assist him/her (cabinet)
decide about the rights and duties of the club members	LEGISLATIVE	establish a body representing the people, make the laws, and control the executive (Congress)
form a body which settles conflicts between club officers and members	JUDICIARY	create a judicial branch which settles conflicts between the executive and the legislative branch of government

This procedure will raise many questions that bear directly on our topic e.g. *Does the election of club officers sometimes become a popularity contest or the choice of well-heeled members?* (cf. choice of candidates for the office of the president of the USA). (see Helms: *USA - Staat und Gesellschaft*, pp. 56-59)
What protection is there for the minority? How can their interests be taken care of? (cf. women, racial or other minorities).
My experiences as sponsor of a "Gymnasium" Student Council taught me that students are almost too eager to change the rules of the body representing them, which raises the question: *Need a Constitution be re-written with every change in the leadership or are there ways to preserve the basic principles while allowing change of detail?*

With the above lists and this question before them, let the students outline a constitution (or statutes), e.g. for an Ecology Club or another club of their own choice. This procedure should prepare them for an understanding of **why** the US Constitution, founded on sound **basic principles**, though conceived two hundred years ago, is still viable and **how** it has in the course of time been adapted to changing conditions.

If you think that this procedure is too time-consuming or beyond the language proficiency of your students, you may begin with a discussion of some of the

quotations (p. 5) or the title of this text-collection LIFE, LIBERTY and THE PURSUIT OF HAPPINESS.
You might again use the technique of brainstorming, i.e. let the students name what these terms mean to them. A couple of students may be asked to find out how these terms are defined in dictionaries or encyclopaedias.

Possible answers:

Life = preservation of life, "Achtung vor dem Leben"
issues connected: death penalty, yes or no
justification of wars
"better red than dead"
abortion
gene-research
Have we a right to interfere with nature?

Liberty Is there a difference between liberty and freedom?
Blanke states: "Liberty" und "freedom" sind im losen Sprachgebrauch synonym, aber im strengsten Sprachgebrauch werden beide unterschieden. "Freedom" ist das allgemeinere Wort und betont die Abwesenheit von Schranken und Beschränkungen. "Liberty" schließt vergangene, gegenwärtige und mögliche Beschränkungen ein und deutet den Kampf um eine institutionelle Verankerung vom "freedom" an. Der Umfang dessen, wovon und wozu der Mensch frei sein möchte, richtet sich vor allem nach dem von ihm erlebten Druck und ist daher von Volk zu Volk verschieden...(1)

Since many young people believe that liberty imposes no restraints on the individual, an excerpt from John Stuart Mill's classical essay *On Liberty* may help them to understand that **liberty** must not degenerate into **license.**

■ Additional text: John Stuart Mill (1806-1873)
Liberty of the Individual.

There is a sphere of action in which society, as distinguished from the individual, has, if any, only an indirect interest; comprehending all that portion of a person's life and conduct which affects only himself, or if it also affects others, only with their free, voluntary, and undeceived consent and participation. When I say only himself, I mean directly, and in the first instance: for whatever affects himself, may affect others through himself; and the objection which may be grounded on this contingency, will receive consideration in the sequel. This, then, is the appropriate region of human liberty. It comprises, first, the inward domain of consciousness; demanding liberty of conscience, in the most comprehensive sense; liberty of thought and feeling; absolute freedom of opinion and sentiment on all subjects, practical or speculative, scientific, moral, or theological. The liberty of expressing and publishing opinions may seem to fall under a different principle, since it belongs to that part of the conduct of an individual which concerns other people;

(1) Zitat aus Gustav H. Blanke *Amerikanischer Geist. Begriffs- und wortgeschichtliche Untersuchungen.* Meisenheim am Glan, 1956, p. 124, Kap. 4 Freiheit, pp. 122-162.

> but, being almost of as much importance as the liberty of thought itself, and resting in great part on the same reasons, is practically inseparable from it. Secondly, the principle requires liberty of tastes and pursuits; of framing the plan of our life to suit our own character; of doing as we like, subject to such consequences as may follow: without impediment from our fellow creatures, so long as what we do does not harm them, even though they should think our conduct foolish, perverse, or wrong. Thirdly, from this liberty of each individual, follows the liberty, within the same limits, of combination among individuals; freedom to unite, for any purpose not involving harm to others: the persons combining being supposed to be of full age, and not forced or deceived.
> No society in which these liberties are not, on the whole, respected, is free, whatever may be its form of government; and never is completely free in which they do not exist absolute and unqualified.
>
> On Liberty

Discuss with the students in what respect "a person's life and conduct may affect others through himself". What is for J.S. Mill the "appropriate region of human life?" and what are the limits of liberty according to Mill?

Let the students give examples of the symbolic use of **liberty/freedom** in the U.S.A.
E.g. Statue of Liberty, Liberty Bell, Liberty ships (freighters used in World War II), liberty cabbage (term that replaced the word 'Sauerkraut'during World War I), Patrick Henry "Give me Liberty or Death", M.Luther King ending his dramatic speech at the end of the March on Washington in 1963 with the song

> My country, 'tis of thee
> Sweet land of liberty
> Of thee I sing,
> Land where my fathers died,
> Land of the Pilgrims pride
> From every mountainside
> Let freedom ring.

A stamp-collector may use his collection and report to his fellow-students about his findings.

<u>Pursuit of Happiness</u> Point out that in the U.S. Constitution this term was replaced by 'pursuit of property'.
What does this change imply?
What are the positive aspects of the 'pursuit of happiness/property'?
(individualism, 'from rags to riches', self-made man, free enterprise = hard work will lead to happiness and prosperity. Negative aspects: extreme, sometimes ruthless competition. One man's dreams may be the other man's nightmare).
For more detailed information see Tracy/Helms *American Dreams/American Nightmares*, Teacher's Book, Section III, Success American Style, pp. 143-194.

It is very likely that in the discussion of these basic terms a lot of interesting questions will be raised. You certainly will not be able to deal with them immediately, but many of them may be of relevance later. Appoint a student to collect them, so you may return to them at the appropriate time.

In case you consider these suggestions too time-consuming, you may skip them at this stage and turn directly to the Introduction (texts 1-4). However, in that case, they should then be used when you reach the Chapter Basic Principles.

<u>Introductory Comments</u>

In order to let the students see these documents in their historical perspective, some background information is offered in the Students' Book. In case they want more information e.g. on the origins of the War of Independence or the deliberations that led to the adoption of the Constitution in 1787, two students may prepare reports. Any survey of U.S. history might be used, e.g.
A. Nevins/H.S. Commager: *The Pocket History of the United States*. New York: Pocket Library. First published in 1956.
J. Truslow Adams: *The Epic of America*. Garden City, NY: Garden City Books, 1933.
A short survey, albeit in German, is to be found in
Erwin Helms: *USA - Staat und Gesellschaft*. Hannover, Fackelträger-Verlag, 6.ed. 1985, pp. 18-25.

Before the students begin analysing the texts, they might be advised on how to approach them. Basic questions to be asked are:

Who said (wrote) **what,**
when and where, and to whom,
in what way and **with what intention?**

When the above questions (not necessarily all) have been answered the students should

identify the **key passage of each text,**
detect possible **biases** and then
summarize the information.

We recommend that students be advised at his stage about the **practise of note-taking,** which will be useful to them as the course proceeds and later, if they should enter an academic career.

● Special Feature: <u>Note-taking</u>

The **file card system** of note-taking recommends itself for this purpose. The following guidelines, adapted from *Bicentennial Youth Debates* (see Reading list) p. 321, should be followed:

- select a uniform file-card size (e.g. 10.5 x 15cm),
- fully quote the source of the evidence on each (1),
- limit each card to a single analytical point,
- quote verbatim where possible (2),
- place an idea heading at the top of the card which corresponds to the argument heading under which it is filed (3),
- organize the cards in the file according to major and subordinate issues (different colors of file cards may be used).

Sample card:
(3) Government based on the consent of the governed
(2) "That to secure these rights, Governments are instituted among Men, deriving their just power from the consent of the governed."
(1) From: The Declaration of Independence, 1776.

As the course proceeds, the students should add other quotations e.g. passages from the Port Huron Statement (text 44).
Up-to-date students might use their homecomputer for the same purpose.

1. The Declaration of Independence, 1776.

If you did not follow the suggestions made for "How to start the course", you could use the comments on Life, Liberty, and the Pursuit of Happiness now and then proceed to the discussion of the other basic statements of the Declaration (see the questions in the Students' Book.)
As an interdisciplinary assignment a comparison with the "Déclaration des Droits de l'Homme et du Citoyen" (1791) or the "Universal Declaration of Human Rights" (1948) - see Appendix - may recommend itself, and the question be asked:
Which document is more radical, i.e. goes further in its guarantees of human rights?
Consult:
Ernst H. v. Bernevitz and Konrad v. Bonien: *Das Grundgesetz verstehen.* Reinbeck: Rowohlt, 1976, pp. 13-15.
Franz Neumann: *Freiheit. Texte zur politischen Bildung.* Baden-Baden: Signal Verlag, 1978.
Wolfgang Hilligen: *Menschenwürde*. Baden-Baden: Signal Verlag, 1980.

In connection with the Founding Father's statement

> ... it is their right, it is their duty, to throw off such Government (Ed.: the despotism of George III.), and to provide new guards for their future security...

Henry David Thoreaus's essay on **Civil Disobedience** might be discussed, not only because in it Thoreau accepted the motto "That government is best which governs least" and even expresses his belief that "that government is best which does not govern at all," but because this essay later inspired Mahatma Gandhi and Martin Luther King as well as the student revolt in the sixties.

Henry David Thoreau (1817-1862), American poet, essayist, and naturalist, a graduate of Harvard University, became famous for his work *Walden* (1854) in which he described his life in the loneliness of Walden Pond nr. Concord, Mass. He involved himself in many social issues such as the abolition of slavery and of taxes, and strongly opposed the U.S. war against Mexico to which, according to him, "the people would not have consented."

■ Additional text:

> Civil Disobedience
>
> I heartily accept the motto,-"That government is best which governs least;" and I should like to see it acted up to more rapidly and systematically. Carried out, it finally amounts to this, which also I believe,-"That government is best which governs not at all;" and when men are prepared for it, that will be the kind of government which they will have. Government is at best but an expedient; but most governments are usually, and all governments are sometimes, inexpedient. The objections which have been brought against a standing army, and they are many and weighty, and deserve to prevail, may also at last be brought against a standing government. The standing army is only an arm of the standing government. The government itself, which is only the mode which the people have chosen to execute their will, is equally liable to be abused and perverted before the people can act through it. Witness the present Mexican war, the work of

comparatively a few individuals using the standing government as their tool; for, in the outset, the people would not have consented to this measure.

But to speak practically and as a citizen, unlike those who call themselves no-government men, I ask for, not at once no government, but **at once** a better government. Let every man make known what kind of government would command his respect, and that will be one step toward obtaining it.

After all, the practical reason why, when the power is once in the hands of the people, a majority are permitted, and for a long period continue, to rule is not because they are most likely to be in the right, nor because this seems fairest to the minority, but because they are physically the strongest. But a government in which the majority rule in all cases cannot be based on justice, even as far as men understand it. Can there not be a government in which majorities do not virtually decide right and wrong, but conscience?- in which majorities decide only those questions to which the rule of expediency is applicable? Must the citizen ever for a moment, or in the least degree, resign his conscience to the legislator? Why has every man a conscience, then? I think that we should be men first, and subjects afterwards. It is not desirable to cultivate a respect for the law, so much as for the right. The only obligation which I have a right to assume is to do at any time what I think right. It is truly enough said that a corporation has no conscience; but a corporation of conscientious men is a corporation **with** a conscience. Law never made men a whit more just; and, by means of their respect for it, even the well-disposed are daily made the agents of injustice. A common and natural result of an undue respect for laws is, that you may see a file of soldiers, colonel, captain, corporal, privates, powder-monkeys and all, marching in admirable order over hill and dale to the wars, against their wills, ay, against their common sense and consciences, which makes it very steep marching indeed, and produces a palpitation of the heart. They have no doubt that it is damnable business in which they are concerned; they are all peaceably inclined.

The full text is reprinted in many anthologies, e.g.:
G.N. Grob/R.N. Beck (eds.) *American Ideas. Source Readings in the Intellectual History of the U.S. Vol. I* (1629-1865), pp. 369-373. New York: Free Press, 7.ed. 1972.
A.A. Ekirch, Jr (ed.) *Voices of Dissent*. New York, Citadel Press 1964, pp.103-115.

Question: *Do Thoreau's introductory statements make sense? Discuss his statements 1. "A government in which the majority rule in all cases cannot be based on justice," and 2. "It is not desirable to cultivate a respect for the law, so much as for the right."*

In order to prepare the students for debating, let them deliver short speeches either on the "majority rule - pros and cons" or the "necessity of obedience to the law."
The following considerations will help them to prepare such a speech:

- Special feature: The Organization and Delivery of Speeches.

- Organization of a speech:

1. the message must be stated with simplicity, clarity and logical consistency,
2. the speaker must decide on the essential points,
3. special care must be devoted to the opening,
   - possible openings: a quotation
     a rhetorical question
     an interesting statistic
     a brief true story
     (in the USA and GB speakers often begin with a humorous story or a joke so as to establish a quick contact with their audience),
4. in the body of the speech the speaker
   must determine the purpose of his speech and which arguments about his topic are the strongest

   must develop a central thesis and select the best two to five main ideas supporting it.

   Such a central thesis presents the main points of an argument in the form of key words.
   As an example the students may, in connection with Thoreau's statement "A government in which the majority rule in all cases cannot be based on justice," discuss the Mercedes company's intention to build a test-course in Southern Germany.
   Main points might be:

   1. the material interests of the farmers/ peasants,
   2. their attachment to the farmland they inherited from their ancestors,
   3. the overproduction of farm produce,
   4. the advantage of such a test-course for a disadvantaged area,
   5. the effect of the cars'exhaust fumes the ecology, etc.

5. the conclusion is as important as the opening:
   it should re-explain the development of the thesis
   it should sum up the main points
   it may end with a final dramatic example supporting the thesis.

- Delivery

  From experiences students have from participating in political meetings, from watching speakers on TV or from listening to a recorded speech, they should list the traits of a speaker that in their opinion make him more effective than another. They will have noticed that voice, gestures, and eye-contact are elements of effective delivery.

Before they deliver their first speech, whether it takes the form of a book report, statements in a panel discussion or of proposing or opposing a motion in a debate, they may be advised to consider the following suggestions:

1. avoid excessive reliance on notes or a prepared text,
2. present a composed, confident image to the audience,
3. speak in short phrases and concrete terms,
4. control your voice
   words must be enunciated clearly
   vary tone and volume,
5. spontaneous gestures and movements enhance the naturalness of a good delivery, but your hands should rest at your side when not in use,
6. keep eye-contact with each member of your class; watch the reactions of your audience. You may notice that they missed a point you made - try another explanation.

(Adapted from *Bicentennial Youth Debates* - see Reading list - pp. 325ff.)

A teacher who wants to widen the topic 'rhetoric'is advised to consult Gert Ueding, *Einführung in die Rhetorik, Geschichte, Technik, Methode* (Stuttgart: J.B. Metzler, 1976), or Heinrich Lansberg, *Elemente der literarischen Rhetorik* (München: Hueber, 1971/4). Peter Bischoff, *America, The Melting Pot*, T.E.A.S. 3, *Teacher's Book*, pp. 139ff. analyzes a speech by Woodrow Wilson ("To Persuade and to Convince: The Use of Rhetoric in a Political Speech.").

2. First ten Amendments to the U.S. Constitution.

In the preliminary remarks to the Students' Book, the question was raised of how it was possible for the Constitution to serve the U.S.A. so well for 200 years - years that witnessed major changes such as the enormous growth of the population, the movement to the West coast, the change from a rural to an industrial society, and growing urbanization.
It was explained that the Americans turned their Constitution into a "living institution" by providing rules about how to amend it. As only twenty-six Amendments have been added to the Constitution since its ratification, it is necessary to point out that there have been other methods to keep it up-to-date. This might be done by the teacher or a student to whom the following comment was made available.
Such methods of adapting the political machinery to changing social and economic conditions include

1. **the interpretation of the Constitution by the Supreme Court**, known as Judicial Review.
Examples are to be found in the chapters "Church and State" and "The Constitution and the Blacks."
2. **constitutional convention**,
the method followed by Great Britain, which has no written constitution and where new statutes replace older ones; this method is also occasionally practised in the U.S.A.

E.g. the two-term tradition = the election of a president for two terms only. During World War II the Americans broke with this tradition (Don't change horses in times of crisis).
The original convention was cemented by the 22nd Amendment.
3. **executive action.**
E.g.a) President Truman sent troops to Korea without waiting for Congress to consent. b) He seized the Steel mills in 1952, because he was convinced that the country's security would be threatened, if the steel workers went on strike during an international crisis.
This case came before the Supreme Court, which by a 6:3 vote held that the President had exceeded his powers.
Text 30 (Bakke Case) deals with the consequences of such an executive action by President L.B. Johnson.

When you discuss these methods of adapting the political machinery to changing conditions you may use Woodrow Wilson's comment:

"The Constitution of the United States is not a lawyer's document, it is a vehicle of life, and its spirit is always the spirit of the age."

The major methods of bringing about changes have been outlined here for use when a suitable occasion arises. The amending process itself is explained in connection with text 22, the Equal Rights Amendment.

At this stage a thorough analysis of all the articles of the **Bill of Rights** should not be attempted. The full text is reprinted here so that the students may refer to it as the course proceeds. The whole text should only be studied if students have already dealt with the Grundgesetz in another course. For this purpose a joint session with the Gemeinschaftskunde-teacher may be useful. If this procedure were followed, the students should look for fields in which the GG goes beyond the Bill of Rights (e.g. § 1 - Frieden und Gerechtigkeit in der Welt, § 3 - Männer und Frauen sind gleichberechtigt, § 4-Recht auf Kriegsdienstverweigerung, § 6 - Schutz der Familie).
If such a comparison is attempted, the students will become aware that the difference between the Bill of Rights and the GG is to a large extent explained by political and social changes that occurred between 1789 and 1949.

Since systematic and deliberate denials of basic human rights lie at the root of many international conflicts, a selection from the Universal Declaration of Human Rights which was approved by the United Nations' Assembly in Paris on Dec. 10, 1948, may be handed out to a student for a short report in class (see Appendix).

At the time of World War II, the U.S.A. wanted to extend some of the basic principles of the Bill of Rights to the whole world, which is borne out by Franklin D. Roosevelt's Message to the 77th Congress.

■ Additional text:

THE FOUR FREEDOMS

Message to the 77th Congress, January 6, 1941

In the future days, which we seek to make secure, we look forward to a world founded upon four essential human freedoms:

THE FIRST is freedom of speech and expression — everywhere in the world.

THE SECOND is freedom of every person to worship God in his own way — everywhere in the world.

THE THIRD is freedom from want — which, translated into world terms, means economic understandings which will secure to every nation a healthy peacetime life for its inhabitants — everywhere in the world.

THE FOURTH is freedom from fear — which, translated into world terms, means a world-wide reduction of armaments to such a point and in such a thorough fashion that no nation will be in a position to commit an act of physical aggression against any neighbor — anywhere in the world.

FRANKLIN DELANO ROOSEVELT

Questions:

1. *What phrases in this Message show that Roosevelt made himself the spokesman of the world?*
2. *Which rights did he add?*
3. *Did he omit any important rights? If so, which and why?*
4. *Was Roosevelt's call for a world-wide reduction of armaments as imperative in 1941 as it is today?*
5. *How realistic are these goals?*

Further information:

Daedalus, Special Issue "Human Rights", Fall 1983, Vol. 112. No. 4. esp. Maurice Cranston "Are there any Human Rights?", pp. 1 - 18.

4. <u>Samuel F. Smith "America", 1832</u>

If possible, you should obtain a record or tape of this song and let the students listen to it. If a record is not available, one or a group of students may recite it. As is pointed out, the tune is the same as that of the British national anthem.
Song books such as *Singing America*, Boston, Birkhead, o.J. (No. 125) give the music.
You might inform your students that Martin Luther King in his great and moving speech at the end of the March on Washington in 1963, to the applause of the demonstrators, said towards its end:

"This will be the day when all God's children will
be able to sing with new meaning
'My country, 'tis of thee...'"

(The text of the speech is reprinted and commented in:
Tracy/Helms *American Dreams/American Nightmares*, Students'Book pp. 58-62, Teacher's Book, pp. 32-33 and 120-132).

Church and State (Texts 5 - 14)

Introductory Comments

There are several reasons why our introduction is followed by a chapter on the relationship between State and Church in the U.S.A.
The students will notice when they look at the First Amendment that the Founding Fathers attached great importance to this issue.
The fact that the principle of the separation of state and church was expanded with the Fourteenth Amendment from the federal to the state level underscores its prominent role. The fact that at the same time both amendments were meant to protect smaller denominations indicates the intention of the lawmakers to secure the rights of minority groups. Dealing with this topic also furnishes an opportunity to introduce the students to the functioning of the balance of power and to the importance attached to the concept that government be based on the consent of the governed.
The **Scope Trial** reveals the power of the states, the case of the **Barnettes** and the issue of **Public Prayer** are examples of the influence of the Judiciary, and the activities of Rev. Falwell's **Moral Majority**, of **the American Coalition of Traditional Values**, and of other religious bodies underline the significance of the principle of "government based on the consent of the governed", 'in the sense that individuals and religious organizations (as, of course, others) are well able to influence political events.
Last but not least, students will notice how principles laid down by the Founding Fathers 200 years ago still have a powerful impact on the current political and social situation. In addition, the relationship between Church and State furnishes a good example of the flexibility of the political machinery of the U.S.A., i.e. it shows how the Americans succeed in adapting the law to changing conditions.
When the students study the table of church affiliations, you might encounter questions about the various groups. Good characterizations of the major religious bodies are found in:
Leo Rosten (ed.) *A Guide to the Religions of America*, New York: Simon & Schuster, 1955 (TB).
Dt. Übersetzung: *Zu Gott führen viele Wege. Ein kurzer Führer zu Religionen in Amerika.* Bad Nauheim: Christian Verlag, 1956 (TB).
A survey of major events in the history of churches from colonial times to the present is offered by
Conrad Wright (ed.) *Religion in American Life.* Boston/New York: Houghton Mifflin, 1973 (TB).
The issues of religious pluralism and civic unity are discussed in:
John Cogley (ed.) *Religion in America. Original Essays on Religion in a Free Society.* New York. Meridian Books, 1958 (TB).
Short characterization of religious bodies are to be found in:
Britain-U.S.A. Now. A Survey in Key Words. Frankfurt/M. Diesterweg, 3rd ed., 1976.
For classroom use: Donald Turner (ed.): *God's Own Country - Religion in Amerika.* Paderborn: Schöningh. T.E.A.S. 18.
When the students become aware of the religious pluralism of the U.S.A., they might compare it with the situation in Germany (percentage of Protestants and Catholics, size of the Jewish community and other religious groups).
If possible you should ask a German exchange student or a native American to report about their experiences with church life in the U.S.A., esp. on such aspects as

1. role of church life in US families,
2. activities of church groups,
3. attendance of church services, and
4. financing of churches.

Such a report should reveal that U.S. churches have to provide their own budgets to maintain buildings and to pay for their ministers and their personnel, i.e. that in contrast to Germany, no 'Kirchensteuer' is levied. Instead parishes have to rely on church offerings and the voluntary payment of the tithe. It is, indeed, remarkable that the majority of churchgoers willingly give one tenth of their income to their church. A consequence of this is that in contrast to Germany, the salaries of ministers vary from church to church. This has the effect that ministers do their best to have large congregations, e.g. by running many activities, such as scout groups for young people, programs for seniors, bazaars etc, which together with the prevalent business mentality explains the fact that some ministers go as far as to "sell" their churches (see text 10, Falwell and the Church Service Advertisements). Lit. Erwin Helms *USA - Staat und Gesellschaft*, Kap. Die Bedeutung der kirchlichen Zugehörigkeit, pp. 156-162.

5. The Scopes Trial

The chief protagonists of this trial were, apart from the biology teacher, John T. Scopes, his defendant, the attorney Clarence Darrow (1857-1938) and, as prosecutor, William Jennings Bryan (1860-1925), a member of the Presbyterian Church and three times unsuccessful contender for the U.S. presidency (1896, 1900, and 1908). Under the Presidency of Woodrow Wilson, he became Secretary of State in 1912, but resigned in 1915, because he disliked Wilson's strong language in the 'Lusitania'- note (the passenger ship'Lusitania' had been sunk by a German submarine on May 7, 1915, resulting in one hundred American citizens losing their lives). The Note is reprinted in Henry S. Commager *Documents of American History*, pp. 102-105.

Though Bryan failed to become president, his influence upon political life was great; he was instrumental in achieving popular elections of senators (17th Amendment), 1920; and women's suffrage (19th Amendment), 1920.

Lit.
Paul W. Glad *The Trumpet Soundeth. W.J. Bryan and his Democracy, 1896-1912.* Lincoln: University of Nebraska Press. 1960.
Lawrence W. Levine *The Last Decade, 1915-25.* Oxford Univ. Press, 1965.
Leslie H. Allen *Bryan and Darrow at Dayton.* New York: A. Lee & Coy, 1925.

Attorney Darrow represented the American Civil Liberties Union. As this organization to this day has been of great importance for the defence of liberty, we reprint a description of its goals.

■ Additional text

> AMERICAN CIVIL LIBERTIES UNION (ACLU). Founded in 1920 at New York City by a group of civil libertarians, including: Roger Baldwin, Clarence Darrow, John Dewey, Felix Frankfurter, Jane Addams, Jeannette Rankin, Robert Morss Lovett, Arthur Garfield, Reverend John Haynes Holmes, Reverend Henry F. Ward, Rabbi Judah Magnus, Monsignor John Ryan, James Weldon Johnson, Helen Keller, Alexander Meiklejohn, Norman Thomas, and Oswald Garrison Villard. Growing out of the American Civil Liberties Bureau, started by Norman Thomas and Roger Baldwin in 1917 to defend conscientious objectors of World War I, the ACLU was formed to counter the activities of Attorney General A. Mitchell Palmer and other government agencies during the hysteria of the red scare.

Often associated specifically with liberal or left-wing causes, the ACLU nevertherless has defended the right of free speech for all manner of groups. It has argued more cases before the U.S. Supreme Court than any other entity except the federal government itself. Famous cases in which it has been involved include the defense of Sacco and Vanzetti (1920); the Scopes trial (1925)... It also succeeded in getting a decision in 1933 that James Joyce's novel, *Ulysses*, was not obscene literature, and it defended religious freedom in *Virginia State Board of Education v. Barnette* (1943), where the latter, a Jehovah's Witness, won the right not to participate in the pledge of allegiance to the flag.
Since the ACLU views political protest as an extension of free speech, it supports the unrestricted right of individuals or groups to express their opinions or to participate in demonstrations. It has thus defended members of the Communist Party of the United States of America, German-American Bund, right-wing Nazi groups, controversial political figures such as Alabama's Governor George C. Wallace, prize fighter Muhammad Ali, and radical dissenters of every era. The ACLU has repeatedly defended the civil rights of minorities and anti-Vietnam War protesters while opposing all government steps such as surveillance, electronic eavesdropping and "no knock" searches, to maintain national security or to interfere with the exercise of constitutional rights (personal liberty, assembly, free speech, and right of petition) to maintain law and order. It won many cases during the 1960s by appealing to the Warren Court.
Using litigation and through initiating test cases, the ACLU seeks to reform society in accord with its own libertarian outlook. In seeking its goal, the ACLU has greatly expanded the concept of individual rights under the First Amendment as against those of society, while simultaneously limiting the power of government to implement laws intended to ensure domestic tranquility. It has done much to ensure and expand the legal rights of the poor, criminals, prisoners, and racial minorities. It has consistently opposed capital punishment, regarding it as a form of cruel and unusual punishment, and has worked to decriminalize such offenses as the personal use of marijuana.

In 1975 the ACLU filed a $500 million class-action damage suit against the Central Intelligence Agency (CIA) and, National Security Agency charging that these federal agencies illegally opened the mail and intercepted overseas telephone calls and cables of so-called dissidents. In 1976 it initiated a campaign to prevent passage of congressional legislation that would stiffen penalties for revealing the contents of secret documents, such as the Pentagon Papers, and conducted a campaign to secure laws to terminate or rigidly control covert operations of both the CIA and Federal Bureau of Investigation (FBI).
The work of the ACLU is financed in part by the dues of some two hundred thousand members located in all parts of the United States. It employs a professional staff at its New York City headquarters and maintains lobbyists in Washington, D.C. The ACLU also has available the services of some five thousand cooperating attorneys who, represent the organization in thousands of cases annually. ACLU policies are determined by an eighty-member board of directors, of which Edward J.Ennis is chairperson; a National Advisory Council, chaired by former U.S. Attorney General Ramsey Clark; and an executive department headed by Aryeh Neier, execu-

tive director.
In 1966 ACLU founded the American Civil Liberties Union Foundation (ACLUF) as a nonprofit affiliate for obtaining tax-deductible contributions to fund its widespread activities. Currently the ACLUF is financing court action in some six thousands cases involving such issues as protecting individual privacy (credit, tax, and medical records); exposing wiretapping by the FBI, CIA, and Internal Revenue Service; fighting censorship by federal and state agencies (including school boards); preventing police brutality; and defending the civil rights of homosexuals, ex-convicts, prisoners, migrant farm workers, and mental patients.
The ACLU, the most renowned organization advocating unlimited political freedom under the Bill of Rights, publishes policy statements, pamphlets, and the magazine *Civil Liberties*.
For more information, see Morris L. Ernst, *The First Freedom* (1946); Lucille Milner, *Education of an American Liberal* (1954); Charles L. Markmann, *The Noblest Cry* (1965); and William H. McIlhany, *The ACLU on Trial* (1976).

Source: *Political Parties and Civic Action Groups.* New York: Greenwood Press, 1981, pp. 22-23.

When dealing with the text you might assign students to read the parts of the interviewer and the interviewed persons or let them paraphrase it and produce it in their own words. If the latter procedure is chosen, this interview may be taped and the performance of the students discussed in class.

As the interview-text shows, the basic question of the Scopes trial was to decide whether the state or local school boards have the right to prescribe what shall be taught in schools and in a narrower sense, whether the teaching of the theory of evolution could be understood as a violation of the First Amendment.
Texts 7 and 8 as well as 11-12 reveal that the issue of freedom of religion and speech in schools is still being discussed in the U.S.A. For some Americans it does not only involve the question of whether evolutionism be presented in school text-books, but also to what extent the question of race, the place of women in society or sex-education should be part of the school curriculum and text-books.
In case information about creationists and evolutionists is hard to come by, we offer the following information:

The *Creationists*, who believe in a special creation of each individual species as an immutable form as described in Genesis, have their stronghold chiefly among the **Fundamentalists** of the Southern states.
The movement developed among various Protestant denominations early in the twentieth century in reaction to the emergence of liberal theology which attempted to recast Christian teachings in the light of the scientific and historical thought of the time. They wanted to preserve the traditional interpretation of the Bible, i.e. the belief in the virgin birth of Christ, in his physical resurrection, in the infallibility of the Scriptures, in substitutional atonement and in the physical second coming of Christ.

Today, they again see their religious conviction threatened and they are therefore intensifying their efforts to bring back school prayer, and to have abortion banned. They propagate the election of Congressmen and Senators who are sympathetic to their goals. (see texts 9-13).
The truth of the Creationist theory was doubted by the *Evolutionists*. Their concept, based on the writings of Charles Darwin, esp. on his main work *On the*

Origin of Species by Means of Natural Selection (1859), embodies the belief that existing animals and plants developed by a process of gradual, continuous change from previously existing forms. (For in-depth information on the theory of evolution, the class may wish to consult a biology teacher).
The Creationists ridiculed evolutionism, because it seemed to imply that man descend directly from the apes - hence the Scopes Trial became popularly known as the **Monkey Trial**.

Lit.:
S.W. Grebenstein (ed.): *Monkey Trial*. Boston: Houghton & Mifflin, 1960.
Norman Furniss: *The Fundamentalist Controversy. 1918-31*. New Haven: Yale Univ. Press, 1954.
M.C. La Follette (ed.): *Creationism, Science, and the Law. The Arkansas Case*. Cambridge, MA: MIT-Press, 1983.
James N. Spuhler *Anthropology, Evolution, and 'Scientific Creationism'*. In: *Annual Review of Anthropology*, Vol. 14, 1985, pp. 103-133.
Edward Jay Larson: *Trial and Error: The American Controversy over Creation and Evolution*. New York, Oxford UP 1985.

The quarrel about the origin of the world remains a bitterly divisive topic in the U.S.A. At present the liberals rather than the conservatives seem to be on the offensive. In the two largest states (except Alaska), California and Texas, the education authorities have been slowly undoing years of fundamentalist influence. In California, for example, the ten-member Board of Education, in Sept. 1985, rejected text-books submitted for use in the seventh and eighth grades, because they systematically omitted "adequate discussion of the theory of evolution...".
As a consequence publishers have revised their text-books (*International Herald Tribune*, Febr. 27, 1986).

6. West Virginia Board of Education v. Barnette, 1943

German visitors in the U.S.A. are always impressed by the omnipresence of the Stars and Stripes. Not only do they feature on stamps, but they are also to be found in every classroom, on all public and many private buildings - not just on national holidays, but all the year round.
The reason is that the flag is considered a rallying point of the nation. As an eighth-grader remarked:

> The U.S. Flag always reminds me of my love and respect for my America. My U.S. Flag reminds me of the freedom that Americans enjoy. Many other countries in the world are not so privileged. The Flag means that we as Americans have the ability to speak, to think, to worship, and to choose our Way of Life. We may even criticize the government if we so desire. My Flag identifies a democracy where people can work together.
>
> From M.G. Mitchell *Propaganda, Polls, and Public Opinion. Are the People Manipulated?* Englewood Cliffs, N.J. Prentice Hall, 1977, p. 35.

In this connection you might also refer to the American National Anthem, written during the War against England (1812-14) by Francis Scott Key in 1812 and long considered the National Anthem; it became so officially by an Executive Order of President Woodrow Wilson in 1916.

■ Additional text: By Francis Scott Key, The Star-Spangled Banner.

O say, can you see by the dawn's early light
What so proudly we hailed at the twilight's last gleaming?-
Whose broad stripes and bright stars through the perilous fight,
And the rocket's red glare, the bombs bursting in air,
Gave proof through the night that our flag was still there;
O say, does that star-spangled banner yet wave
O'er the land of the free and the home of the brave?

On that shore, dimly seen through the mists of the deep,
Where the foes's haughty host in dread silence reposes,
What is that which the breeze, o'er the towering steep,
As it fitfully blows, now conceals, now discloses?
Now it catches the gleam of the morning's first beam,
In full glory reflected, now shines on the stream;
'T is the star-spangled banner! O, long may it wave
O'er the land of the free and the home of the brave!

And where is that band who so vauntingly swore
That the havoc of war and the battle's confusion
A home and a country should leave us no more?
Their blood has washed out their foul footsteps' pollution.
No refuge could save the hireling and slave
From the terror of flight or the gloom of the grave;
And the star-spangled banner in triumph doth wave
O'er the land of the free and the home of the brave!

O, thus be it ever when freeman shall stand
Between their loved homes and the war's desolation!
Blest with victory and peace, may the heaven-rescued land
Praise the Power that hath made and preserved us a nation.
Then conquer we must, when our cause it is just,
And this be our motto, "In God is our trust";
And the star-spangled banner in triumph shall wave
O'er the land of the free and the home of the brave!

At the end of the nineteenth century reverence to the Flag was institutionalized in the *Salute of the Flag* and combined with the *Pledge of Allegiance*.
The Pledge was first recited during the National School Celebrations held in 1892, when President Benjamin Harrison had called for patriotic exercises in schools to mark the 400th anniversary of the discovery of America. The original pledge, probably composed by Francis Bellamy, was changed twice: in 1923 'my Flag' was substituted by 'the Flag of the United States of America', and in 1954 the words 'under God' were added.
As the West Virginia case shows, not all Americans submitted willingly to this practice. As explained in the Students' Book, the Barnettes considered the compulsory pledge and salute as a violation of the principle of the separation of church and state.
As to the **Witness of Jehovah**, it may be advisable to give the students some further information. Students will have observed adherents of this sect in German streets, unobtrusively circulating their magazine "The Watchtower". They might be reminded that the Witnesses were persecuted by the Nazis and still are by the Communists. The sect was organized by Charles T. Russell (1852-1902). Its dogma centers around the second coming of Christ. The witnesses believe that the battle of Armageddon is imminent, to be followed by a millenial period when repentant sinners will have a second chance at salvation.

As this case shows, they refuse to salute the Flag; they also will not bear arms, or participate in affairs of government. Instead of churches, they have meeting-houses called 'Kingdom Halls'. Because all witnesses are considered as ministers of the Gospel, they have no official clergy.
Further information:
Congressional Quarterly Guide to the Supreme Court: Freedom of Religion. Wash. D.C. Government Printing Press, 1973, pp. 962-964.

7. A Legal Battle

Looking at the text and confronting the majority view of the Supreme Court as outlined by Justice Jackson with Justice Frankfurter's dissenting opinion, the students will notice

1. that the nine members of the Supreme Court do not always (indeed rarely) come to a unanimous decision, and
2. that the dissenting opinions are always made public.

They can be told that such dissent may become important when the same or a similar issue comes up at a later date. It may then happen that the Supreme Court reverses its original decision (see text 28); again a proof of the flexibility of the U.S. Constitutional system.
What makes Frankfurter's opinion so remarkable is that he, a Jew, declared the promotion of citizenship to be more important than the religious freedom guaranteed by the Constitution.

8. Newsweek Report on the Lord's Prayer Decision of the Supreme Court

This text is taken from the weekly magazine with the second largest circulation of publications of its kind (1980: 2.9 m, cf. Time: 4.5m, and U.S. News and World Report: 2 m).
American public schools do not teach religion. Those parents who want their children instructed about their beliefs have to send them to parochial schools. A little more than 10 per cent of the children of school age attend such schools. What religious instruction American children enrolled in public schools receive, is a matter of the various church groups; as a rule they offer **Sunday School** before the Sunday service.
Nevertheless, until 1963, it was common practice in the public schools to open the school-day with the recitation of the Lord's Prayer and with a class chaplain, elected by the pupils, reading a passage from the Bible. These Opening Exercises were combined with the Salute of the Flag.
The Newsweek article gives a vivid impression of the reaction of the American public to the Supreme Court's decision to ban the Lord's Prayer from schools. There had already been an uproar after the Court's 1962 decision. The then - President, John F. Kennedy, who as the first Catholic in the White House had encountered great resistance during his election campaign from some Protestant, esp. Fundamentalist voters, had attempted to pour oil on the troubled waters. In a message, he had said:

> A good many people obviously disagree with it (Ed.: the 1962 ruling of the Supreme Court), others will agree with it. We have ... a very easy remedy, and that is to pray for ourselves. And I would think that it would be a welcome reminder to every family that we can pray a good deal more at home, we can attend our churches with a good deal more fidelity ... And I would hope that (all) of us will support the Constitution and the responsibility of the Supreme Court in interpreting it.
> Newsweek, July 9, 1962.

In connection with the comments in the Students'Book that the issue of the public prayer is still fervently discussed, you might point out that according to a public opinion poll more than 80 per cent of the American people favor the restoration of prayer in school (*The Economists*, March 17, 1984). A number of school boards have already circumvented the Court order by allowing "minutes of silence" or "silent prayer", which have been legalized by fifteen states.
Use the illustrations in the Students'Book to show the reactions of the cartoonists.
You might also add that four cases involving religion's role in public life are now (1986) before the Supreme Court. One case poses the question of whether groups of public high school students should be allowed to conduct prayer and religious discussions using school facilities, a practice which is common on college campuses (*International Herald Tribune*, Oct. 8, 1985).
For a summary of the whole issue consult:
Martha M. McCarthy *Religion and Public Schools: Emerging Legal Standards and Unresolved Issues.* In *Harvard Educational Review*, Vol. 55, no.3., 1985; pp. 278-310.
The way in which a religious sect of German origin, the **Amish People**, are affected by this problem of the separation of church and state, is outlined in a text "The Plain People Versus the Common School" in Helms/Tracy *The German-Americans - An Invisible Minority? America in Focus*, Paderborn, Schöningh, 1983, pp. 110-113.
The watchdog function of the Supreme Court with regard to upholding the principle of the separation of church and state appears also in the field of school finance.
One case (Everson v. Board of Education of Ewing, 1947) had to settle the question of whether the First Amendment prohibits the financial support of parochial schools by the federal or state governments. This issue involves, as one can easily imagine, the pocket-books of all American citizens. Should those families who send their children to private or parochial schools have to pay twice - taxes to finance the public schools and fees to enroll their children in private schools? Should all citizens be compelled to help finance private schools?
When the costs of education rose steeply during and after World War II, organizations maintaining denominational or private schools tried to obtain financial support from the government. Reacting to this pressure, the State of New Jersey passed a statute which authorized all school authorities in the state to bear the cost of transporting **all** school children, even those attending private schools. When, in 1947, a private claimant brought court action against this law, the Supreme Court rejected his case by a five to four majority.

■ Additional text: Everson v. Board of Education of Ewing, NJ. 1947
The majority opinion presented by Justice Black:

> ... A New Jersey statute authorizes its local school districts to make rules and contracts for the transportation of children to and from schools. The appellee, a township board of education, acting pursuant to this statute authorized reimbursement to parents of money expended by them for the bus transportation of their children on regular busses operated by the public transportation system. Part of this money was for the payment of transportation of some children in the community to Catholic parochial schools...
>
> The "establishment of religion" clause of the First Amendment means at least this: Neither a state nor the Federal Government can set up a church. Neither can pass laws which aid one religion,

aid all religions, or prefer one religion over another. Neither can force nor influence a person to go to or to remain away from church against his will or force him to profess a belief or disbelief in any religion. No person can be punished for entertaining religious beliefs or disbeliefs, for church attendance or non-attendance. No tax in any amount, large or small, can be levied to support any religious activities or institutions, whatever they may be called, or whatever form they may adopt to teach or practice religion...

Neither a state nor the Federal Government can openly or secretly participate in the affairs of any religious organizations or groups and vice versa. In the words of Jefferson, the clause against the establishment of religion by law was intended to erect "a wall of separation between Church and State"...

This Court has said that parents may, in the discharge of their duty under state compulsory education laws, send their children to a religious rather than a public school if the school meets the secular educational requirements which the state has power to impose. See Pierce v. Society of Sisters, 268 U.S. 510. It appears that these parochial schools meet New Jersey's requirements. The State contributes no money to the schools. It does not support them. Its legislation, as applied, does no more than provide a general program to help parents get their children, regardless of their religion, safely and expeditiously to and from accredited schools.
The First Amendment has erected a wall between church and state. That wall must be kept high and impregnable. We could not approve the slightest breach. New Jersey has not breached it here.
Affirmed.

(Full text: H. St. Commager (ed.): *Documents of American History.* New York: Appleton-Century-Crofts, 7th ed., 1963, pp. 533-535.

If you decide to use this text for a test, have the students sum up Justice Black's definition of the separation of church and state and outline his major arguments in rejecting the request of the appellee.
In connection with the term **appellee** *in this text, let the students form nouns that are derived from verbs, adjectives, or other nouns that designate a person:*

appeal	appellee
exchange	exchangee
refer	referee
examine	examinee
refuge	refugee
legacy	legatee
interview	interviewee
similar: -or	
audit	auditor
torment	tormentor
precept	preceptor
realty	realtor
-ant	
consult	consultant
congregate	congregant
-eer	

voluntary	volunteer
musket	musketeer
-er	
dissent	dissenter
seduce	seducer
crusade	crusader
preach	preacher
-ist	
fundamental	fundamentalist
social	socialist
machine	machinist
cult	cultist

They can use the index-card system (s.p. 12) for such a collection.

9. The Jesus Mania

This excerpt is reprinted from the *Saturday Review*, which at that time (1977) had a circulation of some 500,000 copies. Its readership was mainly made up of well-educated, liberally inclined Americans.
Though the students may find the language of this text rather difficult - the chief reason why we reprinted only part of the article - the case studies with which it opens give the students an excellent insight into the forms overzealousness, intolerance, and fanaticism may take. Students will find that out when they go through the list of words they found in answer to our first question.
The list may run as follows:

nouns	adjectives	verbs
mania	annoying	knuckle under
bigotry	threatening	sentence
pressure	intolerant	
victim	presumptuous	
militancy	pushy	
overzealousness	disruptive	
zealot	coercive	
intimidation	staunch	
pusher		
irrationality		
excess		
vilification		

To make the students see how the author of this article, Dwayne Walls, evaluates the significance of the **Jesus Mania**, we reprint his concluding remarks:

> To a considerable extent, the movement simply represents a turning inward: away from the social gospel and toward a personal, experiential religion that simply makes one feel good; away from the theology of salvation by good works and toward a theology of salvation by faith alone. More disturbing is the persistent element of anti-intellectualism, the retreat from reason back to mysticism and emotionalism. The average, middle-class American church used to encourage discussions of theology and the problem

of faith. Nowadays it is not unusual to enter such a church and hear reasonably intelligent and educated parishioners babbling like radio preachers about Jesus's love and His "presence here among us."
The entire movement, it seems, has one common denominator: an unyielding determination to exalt Jesus Christ and make every living soul his follower. Excesses inevitably accompany the journey toward any such goal. So do internal divisions, and therein lies an inherent weakness in the movement. Christians do not agree among themselves on a definition of Christianity or on what it means to follow the teachings of Christ.
Given the trends in American life, it is reasonable to conjecture that "church religion" might ultimately be replaced by disembodied voices and faces on radio and TV sets. The Jesus movement, with its demonstrated affinity for pop culture, would be right at home in such a setting.

10 Macho Christianity: The Success of Jerry Falwell.

This text is an almost complete version of an article published in *US Today*, a newspaper which first appeared in 1982 and which since then has succeeded against tremendous odds in becoming the second largest daily newspaper with a circulation of 1.4 million copies (1986), only surpassed by the *Wall Street Journal* (1,910,085) and followed by the *New York Daily News* (1,354,220), Los Angeles Times (1,058,698) and *New York Times* (964,360; its Sunday edition claims a circulation of 1,533, 720 copies). (Figures according to *US News and World Report*, May 5, 1986).
In addition to the facts about Rev. Jerry Falwell that can be gathered from the text, the students might be informed that Falwell was born in 1933, became a reborn-Christian in 1952, and has since then never wavered in his fundamentalist belief. He insists: "The entire Bible, from Genesis to Revelations, is the inerrant word of God, and totally accurate in all respects." (*Time*, Oct. 1, 1979). After his graduation from the Baptist Bible College in Springfield, Missouri, he founded the Thomas Road Baptist Church, started a radio program, and a little later a television show.
Today his religious empire includes his thriving church, schools, and a college (Liberty Baptist College, founded in 1972), and many charitable and fund-raising programs. By urging his followers to give at least one tenth of their income (the old tithe) to his church and regularly appealing for cash in his broadcasts, he is able to employ 950 people and controls an annual budget of $56 million. The crusade he started with *Moral Majority Inc.* (recently renamed *Liberty Foundation*) is meant to transcend racial and religious lines.
A few quotations from his sermons may be used in addition to the aspects raised in the text:

"God loves America above all nations."
cf. John Milton "What does he then but reveal himself to his servants, and as his manner is, first to his Englishmen." (*Areopagitica*).
Holding up his Bible, Falwell admonishes his parishioners: "If a man stands by this book, vote for him. If he doesn't, don't." (both quotations from *Times*, Oct. 1, 1979)
(cf. Jim Bakker, another TV evangelist: "We want to see more and more politicians in office who believe what we believe." (*Newsweek*, Sept. 15, 1980)

At the Republican Convention in 1984, Falwell gave a benediction in which he described Pres. Reagan and Vice-Pres. Bush as "God's instruments in rebuilding America." (*Newsweek*, Sept 17, 1984.)

During a service at the Thomas Road Baptist Church in Lynchburg, Va., he asked everyone to stand up if they were 18 or older (= of voting age). He then told them, "You are in the House of the Lord and I expect you to be honest. If you are registered to vote at your current address, sit down. If not, remain standing."
Falwell then had information on where and how to register passed out to roughly half of his congregation that had remained standing. From the pulpit he said: "I don't think I should tell you how to vote, but I do think I should tell you that it is your Christian duty to register and vote."
He then warned them that the same exercise would be repeated at the following Sunday's service and the Sunday after that.
He then packaged that technique and sent it to thousands of pastors across the country.
It is estimated that from two to five million new registrations were the result.
(Source: *National Journal*, Aug. 20, 1983)

After the election, Falwell took credit for the defeat of several liberal U.S. senators, among them Birch Bayh, Frank Church, and George McGovern.

Lit. *National Journal*, Oct. 13, 1984 "The New Right Takes Its Political Show on the Road to Win Power in the States."
US News and World Report, Sept. 17, 1984 "Religion and Politics. Furor Keeps Building."
When you are discussing whether Falwell is violating the First Amendment with his activities, you might mention that during the 200 years of the American republic, church groups and representatives of churches have, for better or worse, influenced political life, e.g.

The stand of most churches in the South in favour of slavery; and after its abolition in favor of segregation; many black ministers like M.L.King supporting civil rights;
such representatives of the National Council of Churches as Rev. W.S. Coffin and Daniel Berrigan leading the opposition against the War in Vietnam; Rev. Jesse Jackson conducting his campaign for the nomination as a presidential candidate from the pulpit, also using it to raise campaign funds.

Lit. Robert C. Liebmann and Robert Wuthrow, *The New Christian Right. Mobilization and Legitimation*. New York: Aldine, 1983.

Topics for discussion or debate

In this connection the question may be raised whether the churches have a right to intervene in such issues as abortion, gay rights, pornography etc. The students may debate the motion "This house is of the opinion that churches should stick strictly to the teachings of the Bible." For this purpose we insert an explanation of the techniques of debating and discussing.

● Special feature: Debating and Discussing

In Britain and in the United States students are introduced to the art of debating and discussing at a relatively early age. Most schools have debating clubs, and state and national competitions (which may lead to a college or university scholarship) are a powerful incentive to excell in this art. Moreover, many Americans schools offer **speech classes** in which students are trained in debating and discussing and often also in play-acting.

This form of oral expression is a very effective way of enhancing the language proficiency of students learning a foreign language. At the same time they gain an insight into parliamentary procedure, in which both forms are used: on a parliamentary motion the government and opposition representatives first present their views, then all members of the House get a chance to express their opinion in the ensuing discussion. Finally a vote is taken. In our suggestions to the various texts we list a lot of questions which may be discussed or debated.

The difference between a discussion and a debate is defined by Webster as

discussion	-talk in which pros and cons of a subject are considered
debate	- formal contest of skill in reasoned argument with two teams taking opposite sides of a specific question.

In a discussion all members of a class get a chance to voice their opinion.
In contrast to a debate such a discussion is much less formal, each member of the group may speak as often as he/she wants, and the end of such a discussion is open, i.e. no decision must be reached.
A debate takes place in a much more formal setting. **A motion** is tabled, always in the form of

Resolved: That ... (chiefly AE) or
This House is of the opinion that ... (chiefly BE)

already indicating that when the vote is taken, the participants must either support or oppose the motion or abstain from voting.

The motion is introduced by the **chairperson** (cf. Speaker in the House of Commons or the Senate or House of Representatives), who then calls upon the **proposer**. In a school debate he should be allotted between five and ten minutes for his speech. He is followed by the **opposer** who is allotted an equal time and who may pick upon the weaknesses in the previous speech.

In Britain both speakers are then **seconded** by another speaker (**seconder** for the proposer and the opposer). They usually get half the time for their speeches.

After they have spoken the chairman **throwns the debate open for discussion**. All the house, i.e. those sitting "on the floor", may now make their contributions. After the discussion, the opposer and the proposer (in that order) get a chance to sum up the debate. They will therefore listen carefully and make use of suggestions that come from the floor or rebut attacks on their arguments.

At the end of the debate the chairman will **take the vote** and announce whether the motion was **passed** or **rejected**.

The didactical advantage of a debate over a discussion is its formalized structure and - a contribution to a political education - the necessity of coming to a decision. This will reveal to the students that they may not fully agree with either side and yet have to make up their minds (just as later on when they use their right to vote, they may discover that no party in an election is 100 per cent to their liking).

As a preparation for a debate or a discussion students may write an essay on the pros and cons of the topic at hand. The presentation of the papers in class furnishes the teacher with the possibility of selecting suitable speakers for or against a set motion.

As experience with debating shows, students, especially German students, often take a debate too seriously by turning it into a *weltanschaulich* contest. It might, therefore, be helpful to arrange a **mock debate** before they debate a motion that lends itself to an ideological dispute. Seemingly ridiculous topics such as 'I would rather be an elephant than a fly' (students usually make excellent suggestions, after they have been informed of the objectives of a mock debate) give the students an opportunity to apply their sense of humor. A mock debate teaches the students to judge the quality of a speaker not only on the basis of his argumentation, but also on his rhetorical skill and manner of presentation.

In British debating clubs it is customary to keep the **minutes** of the proceedings, which have to be read and approved at the next meeting. A teacher may ask a student who is not otherwise too involved to write the minutes.

Useful phrases and technical terms:

to table a motion
to propose/oppose a motion
to rebut, rebuttal
to take minutes
to take the chair
to call for order
to call upon the proposer/opposer to...
to propose/withdraw an amendment
to call to order (if a speaker digresses, is long-winded or unruly, the chairperson may interrupt him/her: 'Stick to the motion!' 'Time, please!'
vote-taking

to cast a vote
to abstain from voting
to raise your hands
(casting vote - in case of a tie, the chairperson has the casting vote - otherwise he/she is neutral)
the motion is carried, passed/defeated, rejected
to adjourn the house (the meeting)

I have the pleasure in calling Mr. X/introducing Mr. Y.
I was flattered by the remarks of Mr. Z.
I congratulate Miss A.
I suggest ...
I feel unable to agree ...
I am sorry to say ...
I do not share the view of ...
May I draw your attention to ...

Literature:

L.G. Alexander, *For and Against* (London: Longmans, Green and Co., 1968). A collection of discussion topics and their pros and cons.

H. Gauger, *Die Kunst der politischen Rede* (Tübingen: Niemeyer, 1952). A scholarly reference book for the teacher.

H. Heuer, "Die angelsächsische 'formal debate'als unterrichtsmethodischer Aspekt der politischen Bildung." *Gesellschaft/Staat/Erziehung.* 12/1967, pp. 40-47.

H.-E. Piepho, "Debating and Discussing." *Praxis des neusprachlichen Unterrichts* 5/1958, pp. 11-15.

J. Raith, "Debating and Discussing." *Der fremdsprachliche Unterricht* 2.8 (1968), pp. 56-63.

See also special feature: *Organization and Delivery of Speeches*, pp. 15-16.

Before debating the motion suggested above the class may listen to and analyze a debate by students of Dulwich College Debating Society "This House is grateful for de Gaulle's Veto" available on tape (36 minutes) through the Institut für Film und Bild, München, IB 2006. The manual (Beiheft) gives the full text and further information about debating, debating clubs and rhetorical devices etc.
The debate should be recorded or if possible, video taped. When the debate is in progress, students should make notes as to the actions and attitudes of the various speakers, the way they address the problems at issue, and their response to hecklers (i.e. to participants who interrupt the speaker with disruptive, confusing or unfriendly remarks). In the replay the students should not only look out for linguistic mistakes, but watch the articulation, enunciation, and voice pitch of the speakers.

Church Advertisements

These advertisements will give the students an idea of the great variety of churches and quasi-churches, sects and fellowships that are active in all parts of the U.S.A.; they also serve as examples of the pluralistic character of American society. The students should understand that their existence is partly the result of the diverse character of the immigrants and partly of the internal division of Christian churches.
Whether this is to be judged positively (as a sign of a "living church", of 'Bürgernähe') or negatively (as "divisive", as a dangerous fragmentation) may be discussed.
Reference to our remarks on p. 20 which explain why American ministers and priests are inclined or even have to "sell" their churches, should be made.

Lit. Malcolm G. Mitchell (ed.) *Propaganda, Pools. and Public Opinion.* Englewood Cliffs, NJ.: Prentice-Hall, 1977.

11. American Coalition of Traditional Values (ACTV).

When **ACTV** was founded some months before the election in 1984, *Newsweek* commented in its July 9, 1984 issue:

> The creation of ACTV signals a new era in American politics and religion. It demonstrates that the leadership of Christianity's New Right is firmly in the hands of religious free-lancers rather than representatives of the traditional Protestant denominations.

Texts 11-13 are examples of how Protestant groups go about influencing public opinion.

Text 11 is self-explanatory as it outlines the character and strategy of ACTV. Two terms ought to be explained:

born-again believer - a Christian who was baptized in infancy, but had an experience in later life that renewed his faith.
He resembles the "elect" or "saint" of the early Puritans, who had to confess in public that they had had an inward experience of regeneration.

secular humanist - Fundamentalists use this term for all those who do not "affirmatively" promote religion, e.g. the evolutionists (see p. 20).

Before you discuss this hand-out, have the students depict recurring, partly antithetical phrases such as:

restore traditional, moral and spiritual values
deplorable decline in the moral and spiritual values of American society over the past 50 years
our coalition crosses all denominational lines
stand united/united voice/united effort
fractionalization, disunity.

12. Ten Basic Concerns of the Evangelical Christian Community

One may wonder whether it is pure coincidence that, analogous to the ten commandments, ACTV propagates ten moral concerns.
In an expanded version these concerns are like Luther's catechism furnished with explanations. Some of these explanations plus additional comments may be used in class. To what extent this is done, is up to the teacher to decide.

ad point 1.
ACTV explains its demand for a Human Life Amendment as follows:

> The declining respect for human life resulting from the practice of abortion on demand has already encouraged a growing incidence of infanticide and could pave the way for public acceptance of euthanasia. At the very least, the federal government must continue its policy of not using taxpayer dollars to finance abortion.

That ACTV's objection to the practice of abortion is based on solid facts is borne out by figures published by the English weekly *The Economist* (March 23, 1985). This magazine based its article on a report by the Alan Guttmacher Institute according to which 83 per thousand white teenagers got pregnant in 1981, i.e. teenage pregnancy happened in the U.S.A. twice as often as in France, Great Britain and Canada, three times as often as in Sweden and seven times as often as in the Netherlands. The abortion-rate was high. Als Illustration: Graphik: Econ. 13.3.85.
With regard to taxpayer dollars used to finance abortion the Supreme Court revised its positive decision of 1973, in which it considered abortion during the first three months of pregnancy to be a right under the equal protection clause of the 14th Amendment in 1977, and ruled that it should be left to the individual states to decide upon this issue. At present ten states and the District of Columbia finance abortions.

■ Additional text: Teenagers in Trouble, The Economist, March 23, 1985

Teenage pregnancy

America the fecund

Many Americans are concerned about the tide of teenage pregnancies, some because young mothers usually have to leave school and forfeit the chance of a worthwhile job, others because they see the welfare rolls rising inexorably with the growing number of single-parent families. Abortions, offensive to more than just the professional "right to life" groups, are also high among teenagers. Yet there are other countries that have been able to avoid this harrowing dilemma. Indeed, America is the only developed country in which teenage pregnancies have been rising in recent years.

In a report just published the Alan Guttmacher Institute, which is allied to Planned Parenthood, compares the rate of teenage pregnancies and teenage abortions in the United States with the figures for five other countries: Canada, England and Wales, France, Holland and Sweden. American teenagers become pregnant twice as often as British, French and Canadian girls, nearly three times as often as Swedish teenagers and about seven times as often as Dutch ones. Why?

Some people are sure that they know the answer. A widely held view is that promiscuous black teenagers are responsible. Not so. They do have a much higher rate of pregnancy than white girls. But white teenagers have a rate—83 per 1,000—that is hugely larger than rates in the five countries used for purposes of comparison. And some of those countries, notably Britain and Holland, have their own racial minorities.

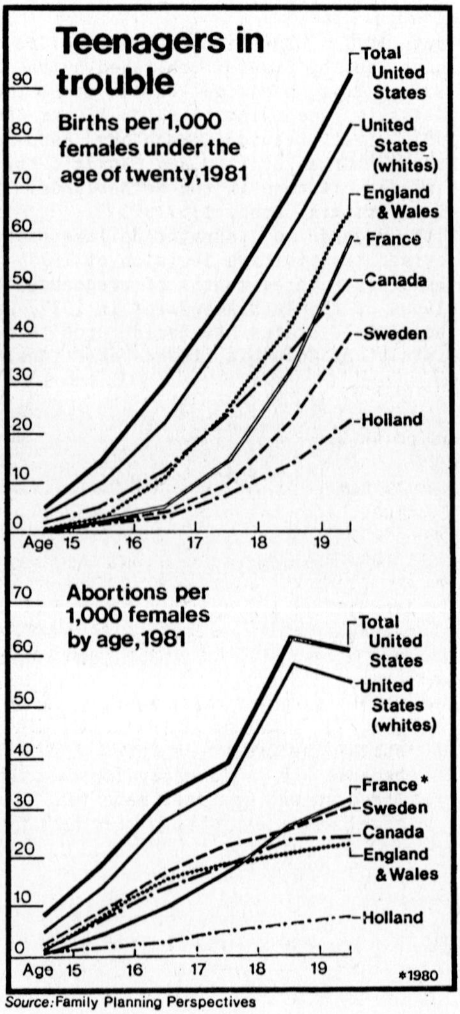

Source: Family Planning Perspectives

Another common view is that American teenagers have babies because this entitles them to welfare benefits that make them independent: a flat of their own and enough to live on. But no again.

In general Canada and the five European countries provide single mothers with benefits superior to American ones.

The study concludes that American teenagers practise the least contraception of teenagers in any of the six countries. In particular, the pill, the easiest method for teenagers to use, is out of favour in the United States because of worries about its dangers; often a pelvic examination, which puts young girls off, is required before the pill can be prescribed. In general, it is harder for American teenagers to obtain contraceptive help than it is for their European counterparts; who benefit from free health services. Sweden, the leader, has a network of centres providing contraceptive care to schoolchildren and the rest of the five provide care free and in confidence. Sweden has been rewarded by a sharp fall in teenage abortions. There are clinics in the United States, but they are regarded as being mostly for women on welfare.

Victoria A. Sackett "Between Pro-Life and Pro-Choice". In: *Public Opinion*, Vol.8. (No. 2, April/May. 1985.
See also: *Time*, Dec. 9, 1985 "Children having Children."

ad point 2.

By maintaining "that religious freedom must be regarded as the first and foremost of human rights", ACTV expresses its full support for the First Amendment. In its comment, it stresses that "Governments, including the Courts, must be careful not to minimize the protection of the **Free Exercise Clause...** by overemphasizing the **Establishment Clause.**
In her contribution to the *Harvard Educational Review, Vol. 55, No. 3, August 1985 "Religion in Public Schools: Emerging Legal Standards and Unresolved Issues"*, Martha M. McCarthy explains the difference between these clauses as follows:

> While the establishment clause primarily is used to challenge alleged governmental **promotion** of religion, in free exercise suits, neutral governmental regulations are usually challenged because they allegedly **impede** religious practices...
> The argument has been made that public school students also have a free exercise right to practise their religion at school...
> (pp. 289 and 290)

ad point 3

It has already been pointed out that reciting the Lord's Prayer in public schools was a general practise until 1963 (p. 25ff).
According to McCarthy (op.cit)

> Currently 16 states have statutes authorizing silent meditation or prayer in public schools, and nine other states have legislation calling for a period of silent meditation. (p. 294).

ACTV expects the Court to nullify its position and supports an Amendment to the Constitution which Ronald Reagan proposed in 1982 which ran:

> Nothing in this Constitution shall be constructed to prohibit individual or group prayer in public schools or other public institutions. No person shall be required by the U.S. or any State to participate in prayer.

This proposed amendment failed by eleven votes to receive the necessary two-third majority in the Senate.
As this text shows, ACTV (like other pro-prayer forces) continues to fight for such an amendment. It also suggests 'equal access' legislation, i.e action by Congress. Such an Act which provides a limited open forum for nondenominational students groups during non-instructional time in public secondary schools became effective in 1984.
For further information see McCarthy, op.cit.

ad point 4.

Of the ten values the ACTV believes in, this is the first with a qualification. Whereas they "are committed to guaranteeing the civil rights of all citizens," they refuse to support "gay rights for homosexuals." In their comment they state: "The federal government ought not inferentially to affirm homosexuality as an acceptable lifestyle, any more than it should affirm a promiscuous heterosexual lifestyle."

ad point 5.

Whilst point 1 and 3 would presuppose a change of the Constitution, in the case of **pornography** ACTV demands action by Congress. Its reasons again, taken from their comment on their list of traditional values, are closely related to point 7:

> Its (pornography's, Ed.) corrupting influence on future generations directly attacks the family, the bedrock of any society... The American public has a right to demand vigorous enforcement of anti-pornography laws.

ad point 6.

This is another point in which ACTV uses the qualifier "but".
Whilst declaring itself in favor of "economic justice to women" (see also 'affirmative action', p. 69ff), ACTV rejects the proposed Equal Rights Amendment (see p. 52ff). The strong wording of the list of values is, however, somewhat qualified in the comments:

> Thus, at a minimum, the ERA must be amended to make it abortion-neutral and to prevent its being interpreted: to require that women be drafted or placed in combat; to deny tax-exemption to religious institutions which treat men and women differently; to legitimatize homosexual marriages.

For an analysis of the on-going discussion of military service for women see: *Newsweek*, Nov. 11, 1985 "Women in Combat? Withdrawing them in a crisis could hamper readiness."
(This article might also be used in the next chapter 'Gender and the Constitution').
See also: Margrit Gerste "Im Manne sträubt sich alles. Frauen in der Bundeswehr." *Die Zeit*, 21.2.86, p. 71.

ad point 7.

In recent years, especially since the Youth Revolution of the late sixties, early seventies, the pros and cons of the **nuclear family** have been widely discussed. Many young people, esp. college students, wanted to and often did replace the traditional family by the **communal family**. Their model was often B.F. Skinner's utopian novel *Walden Two* (New York, Macmillan, 1948)
(If one of your students would like to get an idea of Skinner's idea of communal living without reading the whole book, he will find a relevant passage in: Helms/Tracy *Youth in America*, TEAS 7, pp. 214-216)

ACTV explains its stand as follows:

> The alarming growth of child abuse in our society must not cause the governmental pendulum to swing so far that judges and social service agencies are given excessive, unchecked power over parents and children. Child abuse laws must make it clear that physical abuse does not include reasonable corporal punishment and that mental abuse does not include religious instruction of children.

It thus hopes to restore the nuclear family and prevent excesses by outside agencies.

ad point 8.

Up to the middle of the 19th century, school and college education was mostly church-related. It was only then that free public elementary schools emerged. Today, boys and girls have to attend either public or private (mostly parochial) schools. For parents who prefer to send their children to private schools, this means, as has already been pointed out (p. 26), that they pay taxes for the public school system and fees for having their children attend private schools. To prevent only wealthier parents being able to send their children to such schools, ACTV favors *tuition tax credits*. This, again, would involve legislation by Congress. Apart from alleviating the double burden that parents who send their children to private schools have to bear, ACTV would welcome tax-relief also, because as a by-product it "would be (an) improvement of public schools through competition."

ad point 9.

Discussing this point, its phrasing should be stressed:

> assistance for the *deserving* (Ed.: italics) poor, but (Ed.: another 'but') only through programs which *encourage individuals to be self-reliant* (Ed.: italics), thus strengthening the family rather than weakening it.

ACTV comments:

> Many governmental welfare programs have become part of the problem rather than the solution by trapping people in welfare from generation to generation. Without these misguided programs, many families now dependent upon the government would long since have become self-reliant. We recognize that millions who benefit from welfare are small children and others who cannot work, but government has actually created incentives for able-bodied people not to work, thus making millions wards of the state. Welfare programs should not be designed so that people who want to work have only

marginally more income than if they refuse to work and depend entirely upon welfare.

This stance of ACTV reveals its conservative character and explains its support of the Reagan administration which has in recent years curtailed many welfare programs such as Aid to Families with Dependent Children (AFDC), Medicaid, and the distribution of foodstamps. That these cuts have largely been to the disadvantage of the blacks is borne out by the fact that many of them live below the poverty lines (in 1963 some 20% of all Americans belonged to this category, in 1984 the percentage had dropped to 14.4, but among the blacks, it was 33.8).
ACTV's demand for self-reliance is interestingly enough also supported by leading black intellectuals. Prof. Thomas Sowell of the University of California at Los Angeles argues that programs that were intended to help the blacks have had a detrimental effect on them and in addition developed into a self-perpetuing bureaucracy.

ad point 10.

Against the background of the resumption of disarmament talks between the Americans and the Soviets, ACTV's comment is not without interest, though it does not bear directly on our topic.

> Whereas World War II followed World War I by less than a quarter-century, the United States'nuclear deterrence has for thirty-nine years now protected us against the outbreak of a third world war. Dismantling our deterrence would most likely heighten the danger of war, unless much-to-be desired reduction in nuclear weapons is both bilateral and verifiable. We urge the development of alternative, specifically defensive systems because the doctrine of mutual assured destruction is morally and strategically questionable.

This statement may be interpreted as ACTV's readiness to support Reagan's Strategic Defense Initiative.

Exercise:
After the discussion of the Ten Basic Concerns, the students should list in what cases ACTV recommends
   a. changes of the Constitution (points 1, 3, 6)
   b. actions by Congress or the Government (5, 7, 8, 9, 10)
   c. action by the Supreme Court (2)

Dealing at length with ACTV seemed justified, because its activities reflect perfectly the spiritual and religious scene of the U.S.A., and the present relationship between Church and State.
Seen in connection with the next text moreover,it throws light on the impact group actions in the spirit of "government based on the consent of the governed" do have in the U.S.A.

13. Christian Voice: Report Card

Christian Voice represents a common effort of celebrity preachers to get "pro-moral" candidates elected. At the same time as it mailed its report card to the voters, another 21 Protestant groups and the Catholic bishops issued a record number of voter-education materials.
As indicated in the Students'Book, such efforts have not been without effect.

Rev. Falwell boasted in Sept. 1980 in his sermons: "Senator Gravel of Alaska was ousted last night. He lost the primary. And that is the beginning." (*Newsweek*, Sept. 15, 1980) Falwell was right - before the year was over half a dozen more liberal senators had fallen.
For a summary of texts 11, 12 and 13, a quotation from *Newsweek*, Sept. 17, 1984 may be used:

> If the religious issues of the 1984 campaign carry any lesson at all, it is that American politics has for too long ignored moral dimensions of public policy ... In short, America needs healthy tension between Church and State.

14. <u>The Bishops Call a 'Halt'</u>

For a comment on *Newsweek* magazine see p. 25.
As is indicated in the introduction to this text in the Students'Book, the traditional churches of the U.S.A. are also deeply concerned about Church/State relations. As the Catholic church is the largest single denomination in the country, it represents a political force which cannot be ignored. The Pastoral letter of the bishops, which in its final version was approved by a 238:9 vote, was widely acclaimed for its courageous stand.
The United Methodist Churches (with 9.5m members the second largest Protestant denomination) wired a vote of congratulation: "We thank God for your courageous witness on behalf of peace with justice." Van Voorst in his article "The Churches and Nuclear Deterrence", published in *Foreign Affairs*, Spring 1983, pp. 827-852, pointed out: "The entire spectrum of defense and strategic deterrence is being placed under public scrutiny with a fervor seldom before expressed." (p. 851)
However courageous the stand of the bishops may have been, Van Voorst leaves no doubt that it could

> pose an enormous problem for a church with millions employed in defense industry or serving in the military (Ed.: Catholics make up about 30% of U.S. military personnel) or even, for that matter, for individual Catholics in the highest echelons of governments. (p. 838).

Immediately after the Pastoral letter had been published, the question was raised whether the bishops were really competent to judge such a secular issue. Phyllis Schlafly (see p. 55) criticized the bishops for failing to recognize the dimensions of the Soviet threat. "The bishops are over their heads in a subject they don't understand", she said. (Quoted in Van Voorst, p. 849).
As interesting and essential for our future as the topic of nuclear war/ nuclear deterrence/nuclear freeze is in itself, *Newsweek*'s comment should in our context not be used for a lengthy discussion of the problem of nuclear war or the necessity of deterrence, but as another proof that American Christians of every color exercise pressure upon their government.
The questions submitted at the end of this chapter in the Students'Book will give plenty of opportunity to discuss the issue of the separation of Church and State, the role of the three branches of government and the role of the 'governed'in decision-making.
Lit. Everett Carel Lad "The Freeze Framework", and
John Silver "Apocalypses Then and Now: The Peace Movement and the Anti-Nuclear Crusade",
(both articles were published in *Public Opinion*, Vol. 5, No. 4, Aug./Sept. 1982, pp. 25ff. and pp. 42ff).

Gender and the Constitution (Texts 15-23)

Introductory Comments

At a time when all over the world (at least its Western parts) women are in search of their identity and fighting energetically for equal rights, it is appropriate to look at the American scene, because American women spearhead the movement.

In line with the purpose of this documentation, looking at the activities of women in the U.S.A. will reveal how the Women's Liberation Movement developed, what obstacles it encountered, how individuals and organizations worked on the reluctant public, and how the various branches of government reacted to its demands.

Whilst the previous chapters concentrated chiefly on liberty as an unalienable right, this chapter (like the next) is concerned mainly with the realization of **equality**: equality in politics (the right to vote), and in economic life (equal pay for equal work, equal chance in job promotion - see also 'affirmative action, p. 69ff.). To achieve equality women fervently attack the male-dominated world, the 'macho' spirit which has been prevalent from the beginning of the American Republic (texts 15 and 16). The situation of women in the first half of this century will be illustrated by a scene from Tennessee Williams' Glass Menagerie and a passage from Sylvia Plath's autobiography (texts 18 and 19). The excerpts from Friedan's Feminine Mystique and the National Organization of Women's statement of Purpose (texts 20 and 21) show that today's women claim to be respected as women, want to play a role as females in American society. As not all women agree with Friedan and NOW, a text by Phyllis Schlafly (text 22) is included.

These texts will again give the students an insight into the impact of the American Constitution on the lives of American citizens and into its adaptability to the changing political and social scene.

15. Alexis de Tocqueville: Democracy in America

A. de Tocqueville (1805-59) visited the U.S.A. at the request of the French Government from May 1831 to February 1832 with his friend Gustave de Beaumont in order to study the penitentiary system of the U.S., which was at that time considered to be exemplary for the rest of the world. Their observations during this visit resulted in a report *Du Système Pénitentiaire aux Etats-Unis et Son Appellation en France*, Paris, 1833.

More important than this report is de Tocqueville's *De la Démocratie en Amérique*; 1833, which is still considered to be one of the best studies of American society. The *Oxford Companion of American Literature*, New York: Oxford University Press, 3rd ed. 1956 characterizes it as follows:

> The work deals with the social conditions in the U.S. and the governmental and administrative systems. The advantages and disadvantages of democracies are treated according to their influences on American intellect, feelings, manners, and politics. Generally impartial, the study has taken its place as the earliest important analysis of its subject.

The book is available as PB:
Alexis de Tocqueville *Democracy in America*, 2 vols. New York: A.A. Knopf, Vintage Book, 1955.
For our purpose Vol. II, Book 3, Chapters VIII-XII are of special relevance.

16 The Seneca Falls Declaration, 1848.

The meeting at Seneca Falls in 1848 is considered the origin of the Woman's Rights Movement in the U.S.A. As pointed out in the Students' Book, it grew out of the women's participation in the anti-slavery crusade. When at a World Anti-Slavery Convention in London in 1840 a group of American women delegates found themselves excluded from the discussions, they recognized that the cause of emancipation affected them as well as the slaves.
To explain the fact that states in the Middle West were pace-setters in granting the franchise to women (Wyoming was the first state to do so, in 1861; it was also the first state to send a woman to Congress (1917) and to elect a woman as governor of the state (1927)), you might point out that this region was at the **frontier** (i.e. the borderline between civilization and the wilderness) during those years, and not bound to the traditions which had developed and consolidated on the East coast.
By the same token the Middle West was in those years in some respects a hotbed of revolutionary activities, not least because quite a few of the '48 revolutionists from Germany had emigrated to the U.S.A. and settled in this region after their failure at home.
Under their influence it became the center of socialist groups, e.g. the **Allgemeine Arbeiterbund**, organized by Wilhelm Weitling, and also of groups of women who espoused the cause of equal rights for their sex, e.g. Mathilde F. Anneke, founder of the *New Women's Newspaper*.
Lit. Maria Wagner *Mathilde F. Anneke in Selbszeugnissen und Dokumenten.* Frankfurt/M: Fischer TB, 1980.
300 Years of German Immigration to America. München: 300 Jahre Deutsche in Amerika-Verlag, 1983, pp. 82-83.

Two early influential Women's Associations might be mentioned in this context: the *National Women's Christian Temperance Union* founded in 1874 (it still exists and had, in 1984, 250,000 members) and the *Anti-Saloon League*, founded in 1893. Their activities were chiefly directed at the prohibition of the sale of alcohol which resulted in the 18th Amendment (see Appendix) of 1920. This Amendment was repealed by the 21st Amendment in 1933 when it appeared that the illegal production and sale of alcohol was a far greater evil. This, by the way, is another example of the flexibility of the American Constitution.

18. Tennessee Williams: The Glass Menagerie

Though the students are not expected to discuss at length the characteristics of a play, introducing a scene from the Glass Menagerie will be a welcome change from the mostly expository texts of this collection. The question might be raised as to what extent stage productions reflect and influence the spirit of the times.

Tennessee Williams was born in Columbus, Missouri, in 1914 and died in 1983. His family moved to St. Louis in 1926. After three years at the University of Missouri, Williams worked for a two-year stretch with a shoe company. Then he took up his studies again, this time at Washington University in St. Louis and later at the State University of Missouri where he was awarded a BA degree. His break-through as a playwright occurred when The Glass Menagerie opened in Chicago and New York in 1944/45.
Other major plays by T. Williams are: *A Streetcar Named Desire*, 1947 (Pulitzer Prize), *The Rose Tatoo*, 1950, and *Cat on a Hot Tin Roof*, 1955 (Pulitzer Prize).
Lit. Signi Falk *Tennessee Williams*, New Haven: College & University Press, Twayne's United States Authors Series, PB, 1961.

Marianne Kesting *Das Epische Theater*. Stuttgart: Kohlhammer, Urban Bücher, 1959. pp. 117-122.
Norbert Mennemeier *Das moderne Drama des Auslands*. Düsseldorf, Bagel, 1961. pp. 80-95.

To place the scene reprinted in the Student's Book in perspective, the students might be informed that Amanda Wingfield, who was raised in the South, is constantly reminiscing on her own youth as a 'Southern belle'and wants her daughter, Laura, to be courted by young men. Paying no attention to the fact that Laura is crippled (like Williams'sister), Amanda insists that her son Tom bring home prospective suitors for Laura.
Williams gives the following description of the characters of the play:

> THE CHARACTERS
>
> *AMANDA WINGFIELD (the mother):* A little woman of great but confused vitality clinging frantically to another time and place. Her characterization must be carefully created, not copied from type. She is not paranoiac, but her life is paranoia. There is much to admire in Amanda, and as much to love and pity as there is to laugh at. Certainly she has endurance and a kind of heroism, and though her foolishness makes her unwittingly cruel at times, there is tenderness in her slight person.
>
> *LAURA WINGFIELD (her daughter):* Amanda, having failed to establish contact with reality, continues to live vitally in her illusions, but Laura's situation is even graver. A childhood illness has left her crippled, one leg slightly shorter than the other, and held in a brace. This defect need not be more than suggested on the stage. Stemming from this, Laura's separation increases till she is like a piece of her own glass collection, too exquisitely fragile to move from the shelf.
>
> *TOM WINGFIELD (her son):* And the narrator of the play. A poet with a job in a warehouse. His nature is not remorseless, but to escape from a trap he has to act without pity.
>
> *JIM O'CONNOR (the gentleman caller):* A nice, ordinary, young man.

19. Sylvia Plath: Too Many Choices

Whilst Tennessee Williams chose the form of a play to reflect the experiences of his youth in a one-parent household, Sylvia Plath used the form of an autobiographical novel.
She was the child of Austrian parents, born in Boston in 1932, and educated at one of the best woman's colleges, Smith in Massachusetts, (lately in the news because of a South Africa 'teach-in' with which the students and part of the faculty hope to achieve a complete withdrawal of the College's investments in firms with South African ties), where she received a BA degree in 1955. For one summer she attended Harvard University. From 1955 to 1957 she was a Fulbright scholar at Newnham College, Cambridge, Great Britain, where she got her MA in 1957. Two years later she settled in England and married the poet Ted Hughes. The couple separated in 1962. One year later, Sylvia Plath committed suicide.
Of her litarary Work, mostly poetry, the best known collections are:
The Colossus and Other Poems, New York: Knopf, 1962, and

Ariel, London: Faber, 1965.
Her autobiography/novel *The Bell Jar* appeared in 1953 (New York: Heinemann). She published this novel under the pseudonym Victoria Lucas, because "she didn't consider it a serious work ... and partly because she thought too many people would be hurt by it."
Charles Newman (editor of *The Art of Sylvia Plath - A Symposium*, Bloomington: Indiana University Press, 1970), considers *The Bell Jar* a "testing ground" for her poems. According to Newman, it is

> one of the American novels to treat adolescence from the mature point of view ... It chronicles a nervous breakdown and the consequent professional therapy in non-clinical language. And finally, it gives us one of the few sympathetic portraits of what happens to one who has genuinely feminist aspirations in our society, of a girl who refuses to be an event in anyone's life ... (Ms Plath) remains among the few woman writers in recent memory to link the grand theme of womanhood with the destiny of modern civilization.

Lit. Apart from the above-mentioned symposium:
Stevenson, Anne: *Bitter Fame. A Life of Sylvia Plath*. New York: Houghton & Mifflin, 1989
E.M. Aird *Sylvia Plath*, New York: Harper, 1973

Three passages taken from *The Journals of Sylvia Plath*, New York: Dial Press, 1982, will throw more light on this sensitive poet.

■ Additional text: Excerpts from Sylvia Plath's *Journals*.

My greatest trouble, arising from my basic and egoistic self-love, is jealousy. I am jealous of men—a dangerous and subtle envy which can corrode, I imagine, any relationship. It is an envy born of the desire to be active and doing, not passive and listening. I envy the man his physical freedom to lead a double life—his career, and his sexual and family life. I can pretend to forget my envy; no matter, it is there, insidious, malignant, latent.

My enemies are those who care about me most. First: my mother. Her pitiful wish is that I "be happy." Happy! That is indefinable as far as states of being go. Or perhaps you can run it off glibly, [as Eddie did,] and say it means reconciling the life you lead with the life you wish to lead (often, I think, meaning the reverse).

At any rate, I admit that I am not strong enough, or rich enough, or independent enough, to live up in actuality to my ideal standards. You ask me, what are those ideal standards? Good for you. The only escape (do I sound Freudian?) from the present setup as I see it is in the exercise of a phase of life inviolate and separate from that of my future mate, and from all males with whom I might live. I am not only jealous; I am vain and proud. I will not submit to having my life fingered by my husband, enclosed in the larger circle of his activity, and nourished vicariously by tales of his actual exploits. I must have a legitimate field of my own, apart from his, which he must respect.

Now back again to the present—the mating problem. What is best? Choice is frightening. I do not know: this is what I want. I only can hazard guesses on those poor fellows I meet by saying "This is what I do *not* want." What profession would I choose, if I were a man? Is that a criterion? To choose the man I would be if I were a man? Pretty risky. Occupation? Teacher comes closest now—leisurely enough not to drive me to madness, intelligent of course—hell, *I don't know!* Why can't I try on different lives, like dresses, to see which fits best and is most becoming?

The fact remains, I have at best three years in which to meet eligible people. Few come as close as the one I now know.* I would be betting on dark horses, not on a sure thing. Yet I am disturbed rather terribly by this sure thing. I am obsessed that it is this, or nothing, and that if I don't take this, it will be nothing, but if I do take this, I will be squeezed into a pretty stiff pattern, the rigor of which I do not like. Why not? Ah, I will tell you some of the seeds which will fester in me, sprouting dangerously under forseen conditions:

(1) He is drawn to attractive women—even if it is not to search for a mate: all through life I would be subject to a physical, hence animal jealousy of other attractive women—always afraid that a shorter girl, one with better breasts, better feet, better hair than I will be the subject of his lust, or love—and I would always be miserably aware that I had to live up to his expectations or else someone else would. A woman, confined to the home, doesn't have the opportunity to feed her ego on attractive men.

(2) He regards a wife as a physical possession, to be proud of, like "a new car." Great! He is vain, proud, too. Score fault number one! He wants other people to be conscious of his valuable possession. What? You say, "That is only normal"? Maybe it is only normal, but I resent the hint—of what? of material attitude.

(D. H. Lawrence did have something after all.) And there it is: when asked what role I will plan to fill, I say, "What do you mean, *role*? I plan not to step into a part on marrying—but to go on living as an intelligent mature human being, growing and learning as I always have. No shift, no radical change in life habits." *Never* will there be a circle, signifying me and my operations, confined solely to home, other womenfolk, and community service, enclosed in the larger worldly circle of my mate, who brings home from his periphery of contact with the world the tales only of vicarious experience to me, like so:  No, rather, there will be two overlapping circles, with a certain strong riveted center of common ground, but *both* with separate arcs jutting out in the world. A balanced tension, adaptable to circumstances, in which there is an elasticity of pull, tension, yet firm unity. Two stars, polarized:  like so. In moments of communication that is complete, almost, like so 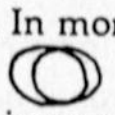 almost fusing into one. But fusion is an undesirable impossibility—and quite nondurable. So there will be no illusion of that.

*Dick Norton in many ways represented a sort of fifties ideal: the serious, attractive boy-next-door who wanted to be a doctor and have a proper doctor's wife. He was very close to his mother—whose sweet pronouncements on the role of woman are immortalized in *The Bell Jar*—who was in turn a good friend of Sylvia's mother.

Exercises:

What characterizes these passages from Sylvia's Journals? (kind of soliloquy, her honesty).

To what extent are her problems related to her nature? Her environment?

20. Betty Friedan: The Crisis in Women's Identity

Betty Friedan was born in Peoria, Illinois, in 1921, and, like Sylvia Plath, studied at Smith College, where she received a BA degree (summa cum laude) in 1942.
Her book *The Feminine Mystique*, 1963, in which she described her deep dissatisfaction with her 'ideal' life, struck a responsive chord among many women in similar situations and soon became a bestseller (24th edition in PB in 1974).
Its publication signaled the rebirth of feminism. In her efforts to make women think of their position in American society, she was soon joined by other prominent women like *Gloria Steinem*, the editor of *MS Magazine*, *Shirley Chisholm*, the black politician, member of the House of Representatives who, in 1972, tried to win the nomination as presidential candidate of the Democratic Party, and *Bella Abzug*, another Congresswoman. In the seventies they organized a **National Women's caucus** with the aim of getting more women elected for or appointed to political office; so far to little avail: in the Congressional elections of 1984 one woman won a seat in the Senate, twenty got into the House of Representatives. Their greatest success was the nomination of Geraldine **Ferraro** for Vice-Presidential candidate of the Democratic Party in 1984. Their hope that women would honor this first attempt to put a woman on the presidential ticket was not fulfilled: whilst in 1980, 49% of the female voters had voted for the Republican ticket (Ronald Reagan), 56% did so in 1984.
Lit. Betty Friedan *It changed my Life. Writings on the Women's Movement.* London: Gollancz, 1977.

21. The National Organization of Women's Statement of Purpose

The fact that the acronym of the National Organization of Women turns out to be **NOW** may be a mere accident, but it expresses also the urgency of their demands (cf. M.L. King's *I have a Dream* speech, which in its central piece also urges action 'now'. See *Youth in America*, St. B., p. 59, "We have also come to this hallowed spot to remind America of the fierce urgency of **now** ... **Now** is the time to make real the promise of Democracy ...).
You might have the students compare this document with the "Seneca Falls declaration" of 1848 and discuss the similarities and differences in the two texts.
To make them understand why these men and women intend "to break through the silken curtain of *prejudice and discrimination* (Ed.'s italics) against women in government, industry, the professions, the churches ...", the following data should be made available to them. (Use an overhead projector!)

■ Additional Text: Data

Occupations of Civil Labor Force, 1980 (in thousands)

	Male	Female
Managerial and professional	13,457	9,196
Technical, sales and administrative support	11,000	19,882
Service occupations	5,585	8,021
Farming, forestry & fishing	2,581	451
Precision, production, craft & repair	12,499	1,056
Operators, fabricators & laborers	14,501	5,486

Source: U.S. Bureau of Census: 1980 Census of Population, Wash. D.C.

Greater Access to Jobs

(Percent of women and minorities in selected jobs, 1972 and 1981)

	1971		1981	
	Women	Black and Other	Women	Black and Other
Physician	10.1%	8.2%	13.7%	14.5%
Registered Nurse	97.6%	8.2%	96.8%	12.3%
Computer Specialist	21.7%	4.3%	38.5%	9.9%
Lawyer Judge	3.8%	1.9%	14.1%	4.6%
College Teacher	28.0%	7.2%	35.2%	9.2%
Elementary School Teacher	85.1%	10.1%	83.6%	11.4%
Bank Officer	19.0%	2.6%	37.5%	5.5%
Bank Teller	87.5%	4.9%	93.5%	7.6%
Electrician	.6%	3.2%	1.6%	7.9%
Truckdriver	.6%	14.4%	2.7%	13.9%
Construction	.5%	22.4%	2.2%	15.8%
Secretary	99.1%	5.2%	99.1%	7.2%
Sales Manager	15.7%	1.6%	26.5%	4.6%
Pharmacist	12.7%	3.2%	25.7%	9.2%

Some fields are called women's "ghettos." Is this changing?

Mothers Who Raise Their Children Alone: 1970 & 1980

(Percent of U.S. families with women as heads of household)

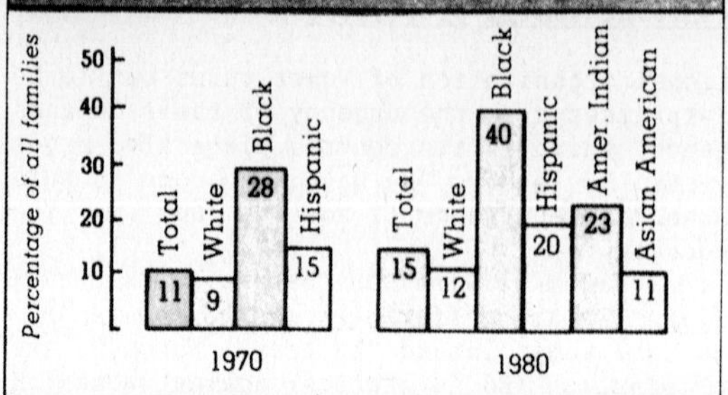

Source: Bureau of the Census

More divorces and unwed mothers shape these figures.

Balancing Act for Mothers: Holding a Job & Raising Children Alone

(The employment status of women who head households and have children under 18.)

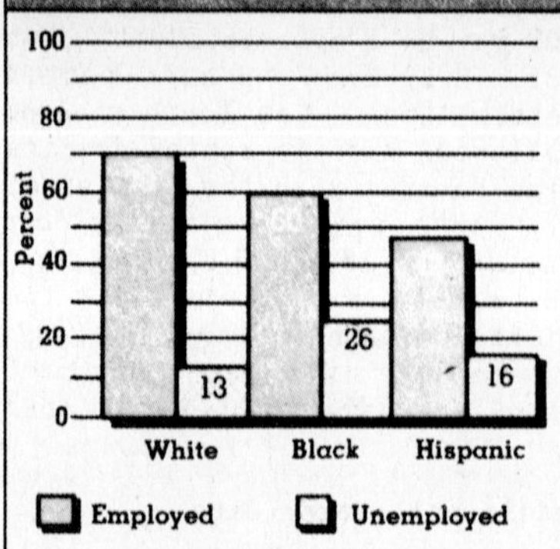

All figures are for March of 1983.

The Wage Gap

(Median income in 1980 for fulltime, year-round workers)

	White Collar	Blue Collar	Service	Farm
White Male	$25,319	$17,726	$14,808	$10,163
White Female	$13,035	$10,685	$ 8,228	$4,026
Black Male	$17,209	$14,486	$12,024	$6,363
Black Female	$12,969	$9,386	$8,350	nf
Hispanic Male	$20,750	$14,328	$11,238	nf
Hispanic Female	$11,913	$9,309	$7,338	nf

The job chart below will help you analyze the wage gap.

The Troubling Link Between Education & Income

(The distribution of family income for blacks, whites, and Hispanics, according to level of education of family head)

	under $5,000	$10,000-$19,999	$20,000-$29,999	$30,000-$39,999	$40,000-$49,999	$50,000 and over
WHITE						
4 yrs. high school	3.7	28.6	30.8	16.6	6.5	4.8
4 yrs. college	1.2	13.9	24.8	21.6	14.5	21.0
BLACK						
4 yrs. high school	12.0	31.3	20.9	11.4	3.8	1.1
4 yrs. college	3.9	22.7	28.1	19.1	9.3	8.8
HISPANIC						
4 yrs. high school	7.0	31.8	26.6	12.1	4.6	1.9
4 yrs. college	3.2	25.3	24.5	19.3	10.0	12.4

Source: *Statistical Abstract, 1982-83.*

Many white high school grads make more than black college grads. Why?

Reprinted from *Scholastic UPDATE*, Oct. 5, 1984

Questions:
1. *How do the incomes of males/females compare?*
2. *How do the incomes of white/black/hispanic females compare?*
3. *In what jobs do women predominate?*
4. *What jobs are usually considered to be especially suited for women?*
5. *What progress did American women make between 1971 and 1981?*
6. *Should advertisements concerning jobs, housing etc. specify the gender/race of a potential applicant?*
7. *Should a quota regulation (see "Affirmative Action", p. 69ff) be introduced?*

Lit. Barbara M. Wertheimer "Women in the Labor Force ..." in: *Dialogue*, No. 2, 1985.

In 1984, 58.9% of all American women worked. This explains why NOW is also asking for a "nationwide network of child-care centers" (s. Students'Book p. 67 Line 8) for "a fair sharing of responsibilities of home and children and of the economic burdens of their support."
Discuss the pros and cons of these suggestions.

An interesting aspect of the activities of the Women's libbers, as the Women's Movement is, albeit pejoratively, called by some, is the impact upon the language.
Just as we have almost dispensed with the term 'Fräulein', so Americans call women in general whether married or not, **Ms.** The term **Mrs.** is rejected, because it derives from **Mr.** We have already referred to Gloria Steinem's magazine **MS.**
Other terms now frequently used are

herstory	for	history
chairperson	for	chairman
congressperson	for	congressman
spokeswoman	for	spokesman

See Cartoons in the Students' Book.

Lit.

Isa Kapp "The Women's Movement Today," in *American Studies Newsletter*, Jan. 1984, No.2, pp. 12-19
Elsie M. Gould (ed.) *American Woman Today. Free or Frustrated?* Englewood Cliffs, NJ: Prentice Hall, 2.ed. 1977.
Barbara Judd/Daniel Josephs (eds.) *Women in the U.S.*, Glenview, III.: Scott, Foresman & Co., 1975
Estelle Steinberg "A Woman's View of Women's Liberation," in *Senior Scholastic*, Nov. 9, 1970.

■ Additional Text: Women's Liberation: A Black Perspective.

[...] In this 1970 newspaper article, Renee Ferguson, a journalist, explains the reactions of some black women to women's liberation.

The women's liberation movement touches some sensitive nerves among black women. But they are not always the nerves the movement seems to touch among so many whites.

At a time when some radical white feminists are striving for a different family structure, many black women are trying to stabilize their families. They are making a special effort, in a great number of cases, to assume the wife and mother role more effectively. Whether a black woman feels that she can relate to the women's liberation movement and the extent to which she is or is not involved in it may well depend on her age and her experiences.

Dr. Anna Hedgeman, for instance, who takes pride in the fact that she lived in Harlem for most of the 30 years she has lived in New York, is a strong advocate of the women's liberation movement. She believes that there is no way in which black women in America are uninvolved in the movement. "We as Afro-American women have to face the problems of total discrimination in our society," Dr. Hedgeman says. "We have had the extra burden of being women. But if you just review the problems that women face you need only substitute the word *Afro-American* people for the word *women* and you have the same problems—job discrimination, want ads that discriminate and false stereotypes."

On the other hand, Howard University senior and Student Association Secretary Pamely Preston doesn't think that the women's liberation movement has any meaning for black women. "As far as I'm concerned the women's liberation movement is trite, trivial and simple. It's just another white political fad," Miss Preston says. "Black people have some of the same problems that they had when they were first brought to this country. That's what we've got to deal with."

In a 1963 article which appeared in the *Washington Post*, the President of the National Council of Negro Women, Dorothy Height, said, "A Negro woman has the same kind of problems as other women. But she can't take the same things for granted. For instance, she has to raise children who seldom have the same sense of security that white children have when they see their father accepted as a successful member of the community. A Negro child's father is ignored as though he didn't exist."

The instability of the black inner-city family has been the subject of concern and study by sociologists for years. A singer, Marjorie Barnes, cites the problems of the instability of black families as one of her main reasons for non-involvement in the women's liberation movement. "I don't think that black women can afford to be competitive with their men—especially now. Competing with them for jobs would just add to the problem that already exists. Black women have been able to find work when their husbands couldn't and have often been the head of the family not because they wanted to be but out of economic necessity."

During a recent interview Height, who served as a member of President Kennedy's commission on the status of women and who has been working actively for women's liberation for many years, explained the lack of black involvement in the movement this way:

"A few days ago we observed the fiftieth anniversary of women's suffrage. But in 1965 black women had to work for the passage of a voting rights act in order to make it possible for millions of black people to have their right to vote protected. I think that it is not that black women are not interested in the liberation of women. But many people have not recognized that everyone has to work for the liberation of black people—men and women."

Perhaps the lack of involvement of black women in the women's liberation movement can best be explained in terms of priorities. The priorities of black women versus the priorities of white women. Obviously the first priority of virtually all black people is the elimination of racial prejudice in America—in effect the liberation of black people. Second in importance is the black family problem of establishing a decent way of life in America as it exists today. When racism in America is eliminated, then perhaps the black family's stability problem will disappear and more black women will be able to give first priority to the elimination of oppression of sex.

Reprinted from Judd/Josephs, **op.cit.**, pp. 173-175.

Vocabulary:

Howard University	a university in Washington, D.C., founded in 1867 for young blacks
trite	too much used, commonplace
fad	short-lived but keenly followed interest or practice
Washington Post	see p. 29

Questions:

In what respect does the situation of married black women differ from that of white women?

Find an explanation for the statement "A Negro child's father is ignored as though he did not exist."

How does the situation of black women affect their attitude towards the Women's Liberation Movement?

For a vivid description of a female-headed black family in Harlem see *Youth in America, TEAS* 7, pp. 92-95, excerpt from Claude Brown's novel *Manchild in a Promised Land.*

22. <u>The Proposed Equal Rights Amendment</u>

de Tocqueville:
"Democratic institutions awaken and flatter the passion for equality without being able to satisfy it entirely."

In connection with this proposed Amendment, the amending process should be explained.
The procedure is laid down in Article V of the Constitution (see Appendix). It says in short that

whenever 2/3 of both Houses (Senate and House of Representatives) or
2/3 of the legislatures of the States
propose an Amendment and
3/4 of the States (=38) ratify it,
such an Amendment will be added to the Constitution.

(cf. Germany: Article 79 of the Grundgesetz demands a 2/3 majority of the Bundestag **and** the Bundesrat).
As the case of ERA shows, it is not easy to find these majorities in both Houses of Congress and in the States. Though ERA passed the House of Representatives by a vote of 354 : 23, and the Senate by 84 : 8, it did not find the necessary majority in the States.
It can be assumed that the Founding Fathers erected this hurdle

1. because it stresses the federal character of the U.S.A., i.e. they deemed it necessary that virtually **all** states cooperated, and
2. because they wanted to underscore the principle of the division of powers.

One of the consequences of this ruling has been that comparatively few (26) Amendments have been added to the Constitution since 1787.

In the discussion about ERA the nation was and is divided. It had the full support of most women's organizations (NOW, the League of Women Voters, the Homemakers of America and the Women's Christian Temperance Union, most of the Trade Unions affiliated to the AFL/CIO and of many Democrats).
Such conservative groups as the Daughters of the American Revolution, the John Birch Society, the American Independent Party, the KuKluxKlan and the Young Americans for Freedom, and (perhaps surprisingly) the American Communist Party rejected it.
(More details on these organizations can be found in Helms *U.S.A. Staat und Gesellschaft*).
Phyllis Schlafly (see p. 55), the founder of the Eagle Forum, organized a **STOP ERA** campaign.
(see also Chapter Church and State, ACTV.)
<u>Lit.</u>
Emily and P.O. d'Aulaire "ERA - What's it all about," in *Reader's Digest*, Febr. 1977, pp. 98-102.

A speech by the Republican Senator, James L. Buckley of New York, one of the eight Senators who voted against the adoption of the ERA by Congress, contains some of the issues brought forward by opponents of this Amendment.

■ Additional Text:

The Equal Rights Amendment:
Senator James L. Buckley's Speech in the Senate, 1972.

I find myself in full agreement with the finding that there still exists in our country a discrimination against women which cannot be justified and which ought not to be tolerated. The argument, therefore, concerns only the question of how best to redress these legitimate grievances.

In America today we find three factors which affect the relative rights, privileges, duties, immunities, and obligations of men and women. Some of these are cultural, others social, and the balance economic. I speak of distinctions based on sex, deferences conferred because of sex, and discrimination which is predicated on sex. Only the last, I submit, is the proper target of the amendment now under consideration and of the enormous effort by the women of America to redress their longstanding and legitimate grievances. Yet the proposed equal rights amendment would have the inevitable effect of eliminating all of these differentiations—these distinctions, deferences, and discriminations—in the name of an abstract equality, of whether they in fact infringe upon the real rights of women.

It is because of this—because, quite specifically, of my deep respect for women—that I cannot support the amendment. And I cannot support it because whatever the intentions of its sponsors, I think we will inevitably find it tugged and twisted and extended far beyond the limits of common sense and reason. I am opposed to the proposed amendment because, in its attempt to eliminate discrimination against women, it will at the same time inevitably strike down those distinctions and those deferences which our society now extends to women.

I am further convinced that adequate remedies exist today to correct the inequities which are the appropriate targets for a women's rights amendment. Thus I am encouraged in the belief that a case-by-case approach will produce beneficial results.

The most conspicuous and outspoken representatives of the women's liberation movement have a habit of talking as if they were the duly appointed guardians of the women of America. Whether the women of America want or need this kind of guardianship, however, is another matter altogether. I am unaware of any vote granting representative authority to the women's liberation movement from the women of America. Nor am I aware of any demonstrable indication that the women of America approve of what their self-appointed guardians would have delivered up for them. On the contrary, as the distinguished Senator from North Carolina [Sam Ervin] has pointed out, in the only detailed poll taken on the subject, the overwhelming majority of those polled revealed a singular indifference, if not hostility, toward the more obvious legal consequences that would flow from the passage of the equal rights amendment. Fully 77 percent of American women opposed equal treatment with respect to military service. Some 83 percent opposed the idea that a wife should be the breadwinner if she were a better wage earner than her husband. And 69 percent opposed the idea that a woman should pay alimony if she has money and her husband does not.

Yet, if the equal rights amendment were to be ratified, women would be drafted and could be required to serve in combat. States would be barred from imposing greater liability for support on a husband than on a wife merely because of his sex. Criminal sanctions for failure to support one's family could not be sustained where only the male is liable for such support. And obligation for alimony could be placed upon either spouse. Such changes in the law may bring joy to the hearts of the more militant advocates of the women's liberation movement. But they are not necessarily in the interests of most American women.

I not only believe that the great majority of American women find fulfillment in their roles as wives and mothers, but I suspect that the great majority of American women are inclined to resent the demeaning, derogatory, and cynical posture taken against marriage and motherhood by some of the outspoken advocates of the women's liberation movement, as if marriage and motherhood were the hallmarks of inferiority and servitude. To be sure, not all feminists share this jaundiced view, a fact for which we can all be thankful. There are many articulate and engaging activists in the movement, and they have made a compelling case for altering many of our laws which unjustly discriminate against women, especially in the area of job opportunities. With many of their grievances I am in great sympathy. But I am satisfied that present constitutional and statutory law provide ample opportunities for redress. I am not at all convinced that the "liberation" of some women requires the removal of legal protections from others or the imposition of greater legal burdens upon those who do not share the goals of the liberationists.

Vocabulary

redress a grievance	put right an unjust treatment
deference	showing respect for another's wishes
predicate	state as being necessary/true
target	goal
infringe	violate (rights etc.)
tug	a sudden pull
inequity	injustice, unfairness
conspicuous	easily seen
hostility	enmity, unfriendliness
alimony	dt. Alimente
be drafted	AE called to military service
spouse	husband or wife
demeaning	insulting, undignified
derogatory	showing lack of respect
hallmark	symbol/sign of excellence
jaundiced	prejudiced, critical
articulate	able to express thoughts/feelings clearly.

1. *What do you think Buckley meant when he talked about "distinctions based on sex" and "deferences conferred because of sex"?*
2. *Do you agree with Buckley that the ERA "will strike down those distinctions*

and those deferences"? Explain your standpoint.

3. *Would you side with those women who oppose military service for women, alimony payments by women, mixed sports and making women the breadwinners?*
4. *Are there points with which you agree as well as those with which you disagree? Explain your views.*
5. *Draft a* **letter** *to a magazine or newspaper editor or to Senator Buckley explaing why you are in favour of or against ERA and agree or disagree with his arguments.*
6. *Debate: This House views with alarm the time when the women of this generation will be the mothers of the next, or This House rejects (supports) military service for women.*

The Proposed Equal Rights Amendment
MS Interview with Phyllis Schlafly.

P. Schlafly, born in 1925, is an ultra-conservative who has been fighting ERA since 1972. Since then she has testified before thirty state legislatures and, as President of the **Eagle Forum**, a national pro-family organization, at Hearings before the Subcommittee on Compensation and Employee Benefits of the House of Representatives.
Schlafly studied political science and law and got degrees from Washington University and Radcliffe College.
She has published a number of books and pamphlets, such as *A Choice not an Echo*, 1964, a tract to boost the Republican presidential candidate of that year, Barry Goldwater - it sold 3 million copies; *Strike from Space*, in which she deals with the possibility of a nuclear attack by the USSR, and *Safe not Sorry*. She also publishes *The Phyllis Schlafly Report*, a newsletter.

She is the wife of an attorney, and mother of six children. To the disgust of the Women's Movement, she calls herself chair**man** of STOP ERA, and identifies herself as **Mrs.** (not Ms.) Schlafly. She sought public office several times (for Congress in 1952 and 1970) and for the presidency of the National Federation of Republican Women, but was never successful.
Her opposition to ERA; child care centers; abortion, gay rights, and pornography may be compared with the program of NOW and the ACTV.
To round up the portrait of this woman, here are three quotations, one from an interview with *Rolling Stone*, Nov. 26, 1981, in which she described the atomic bomb as "a gift to our country by a wise God." Another from an earlier interview with *MS* correspondents:

> The truth is that American women have never had it so good. Why should we lower ourselves to 'equal rights' when we already have the status of special privilege,

and a third from *McCall's*:

> A woman should spend the first twenty years of her life growing up, the next twenty raising the next generation and the third saving the world.

Lit.

Henry Schipper: "Some Girls Checking in With Phyllis Schlafly." In: *Rolling Stone*, Nov. 26, 1981.
Lisa Cronin Wohl "Phyllis Schlafly. 'The Sweetheart of the Silent Majority'". In: *MS*, March 1974.
Barbara G. Harrison "The Woman is Fighting the Law that Most Women Want." *McCall's*, April 1982.

Thomas I. Emerson, Gail Falk et al. "The ERA: A Constitutional Basis for Equal Rights for Women." *Yale Law Journal*, April 1982, 7) (a landmark article about the legal aspects of ERA).

23. A humorous Commentary on the Feminist Movement

This text speaks for itself and needs no comment.

Summarizing the chapter, the following questions in addition to those mentioned in the Student's Book may be raised:

What economic and political circumstances contributed to the achievements of women in the U.S.A.?
(The widespread affluence and the desire of those less affluent to 'Do as the Joneses do,' the persuasion of the media, the years of full employment which gave women a chance to find a job; the Civil Rights Movement with its demand for more equality, the Students' Movement, the role of women during the two World Wars).

What part was played by the three branches of government?
Which branch was most active in securing equal rights for women?

How effective were the activities of individuals and groups?

How does the U.S. Women's Movement compare with its German counterpart? (Helene Lange, Clara Zetkin, Gertrud Bäumer, Alice Schwarzer, Jutta Ditfurth and others).

The Constitution and the Black People (Texts 24-31)

Introductory Comments

This chapter focusses on the reference to the black population in the Constitution, upon legislation concerning the Blacks, and on activities of the American people (white and black) to realize Civil Rights for **all** citizens of the U.S.A.
Since the events leading to the Civil War (1861-1865) have to be understood in order to understand what followed it, the preliminary remarks in the Students' Book should be discussed from the following points of view:

How did the 'peculiar institution'(=slavery) come about?
It should be stressed
1. *that the blacks in contrast to the white immigrants came to America against their will, that they chiefly worked as slaves on the cotton fields of the South, after attempts to employ the native Americans (the Indians) had failed;*
2. *that early attempts to abolish slavery on moral and religious grounds had failed, and that formidable resistance only developed in the first half of the nineteenth century;*
3. *that Abraham Lincoln succeeded in preventing the break-up of the Union by defeating the slave-holding states of the South, which earned him the title "Savior of the Union".*

For further information consult:
Erwin Helms *America Today. Black America.* Tübingen; Deutsches Institut für Fernstudien, 1985.
esp. p. 11 "Resolution of the Germantown Mennonites."
p. 12 "The Constitution of the American Anti-Slavery Society."
pp. 13-15 "Lincoln's change in his attitude toward slavery between 1858 and 1864."

Lit.
Don E. Fehrenbacher "Race and Slavery in the American Constitutional System, 1787-1864". In: *this Constitution*, No. 4, Fall 1984, pp. 12-27. Wash. D.C.

24. The Emancipation Proclamation, 1863

This text provides the first example in this collection of the direct influence of the Executive on matters of state.
Students should take note of the wording of the Proclamation:
"I, Abraham Lincoln" and the repeated use of the personal pronoun "I", and also that Lincoln acted on the power "vested in him" as the **Commander-in-Chief** of the Army and Navy of the U.S. (Constitution Article 2, Section 2).
The President's power as Commander-in-Chief has been of great consequence in American history. Some examples:

> President Truman used it when he sent troops to Korea (1950) and when, in 1952, he ordered the Secretary of Commerce to take over and operate the steel mills on the ground that a strike (which was threatening) would jeopardize national security; an action which the Supreme Court declared to have been unconstitutional.
>
> During the War in Vietnam again various presidents took action on the basis of their Commander-in-Chief function. When it turned out

that this had led to the "Imperial Presidency" of Richard M. Nixon, Congress, with the **War Powers Act** of 1973, limited the President's power by determining that no president may send troops to foreign countries for more than sixty days without the consent of Congress.

When discussing the final paragraph of the Proclamation, it should be pointed out how skilfully Abraham Lincoln combined the material interests of the Union ("persons of suitable conditions will be received into the armed services of the U.S.") with moral principles ("act of justice," "I invoke the considerate judgment of mankind and the gracious favor of Almighty God.")
The students might also be informed that on the occasion of the **March on Washington** in 1963 (the 100th anniversary of this Proclamation), Martin Luther King, in his moving speech, referred to the promises of this Proclamation.
One student might be asked to read King's speech and report to the class in greater detail of how King appealed to his nation to fulfil the promises of the Declaration of Independence and this Proclamation.
The text of the speech is reprinted in Tracy/Helms *American Dreams/American Nightmares*, pp. 58-62. If available, the Teacher's Book to this text-collection should be handed out to the reporting student.
The following cassette and film, available through the Amerika-Häuser, may also be used:

"We shall overcome." A Documentary of the March on Washington with the complete speech by M.L. King.
The March. A film - also suitable for listening comprehension.

25. The Thirteenth, Fourteenth, and Fifteenth Amendments

When these Amendments are analysed, special attention should be paid to the following passage of the **Fourteenth Amendment**:

> No State shall make or enforce any law which shall abridge the privileges or immunities of citizens of the U.S.; nor shall any State deprive any person of life, liberty or property, *without due process of law*; nor deny to any person within its juridiction the *equal protection of the law* (Ed.'s italics).

The students should understand that this clause extends principles that, according to previous regulations of the Constitution (e.g. the separation of Church and State), were applied to the federal republic only, but which were henceforth also applicable to the States.
The emphasis put on the rule of law (due process of law) within the Republic was just as important. As has already been pointed out, women referred to this clause in their demands for equal rights. It also played an important role during the 'witchhunts'of Senator McCarthy in the fifties (Arthur Miller alluded to them in his play *The Crucible*).
Since other Amendments also end with the phrase: "The Congress shall have power to enforce this article by appropriate legislation," it may be useful to explain the significance of this phrase, i.e. that the Constitution fixes the general outlines of a policy, which is then implemented by Congress.

26. The Civil Rights Act of 1875

This Act furnishes a good example of a transfer of the principles of the 13th-15th Amendments into legislation by Congress.

As pointed out in the Students' Book, white racists in the South were successful after the Reconstruction Period, 1865-1877, when troops of the North had occupied the South, in practically restoring the blacks to a condition which did not differ much from the situation they were in during slavery.
In the study letter **America Today-Black America** (see Bibliographies p. 105) you will find more information about Literacy Tests, and the Poll Tax.

■ Additional Text: One Negro who's not going to vote.

A Negro went to register. The white man taking his application gave him the standard literacy tests: "What is the first line of the 32nd paragraph of the United States Constitution?" - The applicant answered correctly. "Name the eleventh President of the United States and his entire cabinet." - The applicant answered perfectly. Finally, unable to trip him up, the white man asked, "Can you read and write?" The applicant wrote his name and then was handed a newspaper in Chinese to test his reading. He studied it carefully for a time. "Well, can you read it?" - "I can read the headline, but I can't make out the body text." - Incredulous, the white man said: "You can read t h a t headline?" - "Oh yes, I've got the meaning all right." - What's it say?" - "It says this is one negro in Mississipppi who's not going to vote this year."

(John Howard Griffin)

How successful the Southerners were in preventing the implementation of this Act is evident when you read the **Civil Rights Act** of 1964: it again guaranteed the Blacks those rights which they had been promised in 1875 (see the above-mentioned study letter *Black America*, pp. 22-23).

27. <u>Intimidation of the Black Population</u>
<u>Leaflet of the Ku Klux Klan</u>

Ever since the Ku Klux Klan was founded in 1865, it has harassed and intimidated the black population of the U.S.A.
A passage from *Keesing's Research Report: Race Relations in the U.S.A., 1954-1968*, sums up the history of the KKK:

> The original Ku Klux Klan was founded in Tennessee in 1865 as a social club; the name derived from the Greek **kyklos** (circle), 'klan'being added for alliteration. It rapidly developed into a political organization aimed at restoring white supremacy in the South by terrorizing the newly emancipated and enfranchised Negroes, and was stamped out in 1871 under special legislation introduced by President Grant. It was revived in Georgia in 1915 as an anti-Negro, anti-Jewish, anti-Catholic, anti-foreign, and anti-labor organization, and between 1920 and 1924 grew into a nation-wide movement with between 4,000,000 and 5,000,000 members, which politically dominated the Southern States, Indiana, Colorado, and Oregon. Its influence declined after 1926; it was discredited by the discovery in 1939 of its link with the pro-Nazi **German-American Bund**, and was formally disbanded in 1944 when the government tried to collect unpaid taxes.

> It was revived again soon after by Dr. Samuel Green, an Atlanta surgeon, who died in 1949 (p. 7).

About the activities of the Ku Klux Klan, W.J. Cash wrote in his book *The Mind of the South*, Garden City, NY: Doubleday Anchor Books, 1954:

> Here in ghostly rides through the moonlit, aromatic evening to whip a Negro or a prostitute or some poor white given to violating the Seventh Commandment or drinking up his scant earnings instead of clothing his children, or merely given to staying away from church; to tar and feather a labor organizer or a schoolmaster who had talked his new ideas too much - in slow, swaying noonday parades through the burning silence of towns where every Negro was gone from the streets..., here was surcease for the personal frustrations and itches of the Klansman... (p. 337).

After the Supreme Court had ruled in 1954 that segregation in schools was unconstitutional (see text 28), not only did the Ku Klux Klan resume its Negro baiting with new intensity, but another organization, the **White Citizens Council** (its first branch was founded in Indianola, Mississippi, in July 1954) joined the anti-desegregation campaign.
Martin Luther King, in his book *Where Do We Go from Here?*, New York: Beacon Books; London: Penguin Books, 1968, described these Councils in the following terms:

> Since they occasionally recruit members from a higher social and economic level than the Klan, a halo of partial respectability hovers over them. But like the Klan they are determined to preserve segregation despite the law. Their weapons of threat, intimidation, and boycott are directed both against Negroes and against any whites who stand for justice... .
> The Citizens Councils often argue piously that they abhor violence, but their defiance of the law, their unethical methods, and their vitriolic pronouncements inevitably create the atmosphere in which violence thrives.

For further information:
Daniel J. Rothman/Sheila M. Rothman (eds.) *Sources of the American Social Tradition*, Vol. II, Chapt. 17 "The Ku Klux Klan", New York: Basic Books, 1975.

■ Additional Text: Leaflet of the White Citizens Council

> When, in the course of human events, it becomes necessary to abolish the Negro race, proper methods should be used. Among these are guns, bows and arrows, sling shots and knives.
> We hold these truths to be self-evident, that all whites are created equal with certain rights; among them are Life, Liberty and the Pursuit of Dead Niggers.
> In every stage of the bus boycott we have been oppressed and degraded because of black, slimy, juicy, unbearable, stinking niggers. The conduct should not be dwelt upon them because they have an ancestral background of Pigmies, headhunters and snot suckers. My friends, it is time we wised up these black devils. I tell you they are a group of two-legged agitators who persist in walking up and down our streets protruding their black lips. If we don't stop helping these African flesh eaters, we will soon wake up and find Rev. King in the White House.
> *Let's Get on the Ball, White Citizens.*

Source: John B. Martin *The Deep South says Never*, New York: Ballantine Books, 1957.

The form of this leaflet clearly reveals the bigotry of the White Citizens Council. By using the 'sacred' words of the Declaration of Independence ("When in the course of time ... We hold these truth to be self-evident") they try to camouflage their gruesome morale.
Have the students analyse this text and comment on it.
Explain the words snot - mucus in the nose; wised up - make them understand.

Questions:
1. *What do these passages and the leaflet in the Students' Book tell you about the goals and methods of the KKK and the Citizens Councils?*
2. *What are the political and psychological motives of these groups?*
3. *What layers of American society supported them?*
4. *For what reasons, do you think, did the clergy of the South often side with the KKK? Remember that a church tax is not levied in the U.S.A. and that churches and their ministers depend on the individual contributions of their congregations.*

<u>Claude McKay: The Lynching</u>

Claude McKay (1891-1948) was born in a village on the Island of Jamaica. He came to the U.S.A. in 1912, attended the then all-black Tuskegee Institute and later Kansas State University. He eventually became the Associate Editor of **The Liberator**. He travelled widely and spent almost ten years in Europe.
Before the class analyses and interprets the poem, they may be offered the following definition of the term **lynching**:

> **Lynching**, extralegal infliction of capital punishment by a self-constituted group. ... American pioneers whose settlements had not yet established legal institutions frequently were forced to take the law in their own hands. ... Crimes that seemed to them capital, such as rape, were punished by lynching. Horse stealing and cattle rustling were such crimes, since often pioneers (notably cowboys) who lost their horses and cattle thereby lost their livelihood.
> In the chaotic social conditions of the South during Reconstruction days there was considerable resort to lynching, particularly by the Ku Klux Klan. The tradition of using violence against Negroes accused of serious crime (especially of rape of a white woman or murder of a white man) was maintained in the period after Reconstruction to maintain "white supremacy".
>
> Source: *The Columbia Encyclopedia*, New York: Columbia University Press, 3rd edit. 1963.

According to records kept by the Tuskegee Institute, 1992 Americans have been lynched since 1900 (196 whites and 1796 blacks), mostly for rape, but also for horse and cattle stealing. The annual cases of lynching have dropped to between nil and three since 1952. (see also the Chapter "the right to bear arms").
The discussion of the sonnet should evolve around McKay's skill in evoking the mood of the blacks and the whites and on the imagery he uses (e.g. the Northern star - which pointed the way to freedom and guided the fugitive from slavery to the free North along the underground railroad, the semi-legendary local groups of Northern abolitionists both white and Negro, who assisted fugitives to escape).

Lit.

Larry Gara *The Liberty Line.* 1961

Peter Noçon *The English Sonnet.* TEAS 5; Paderborn: Schöningh, Students' Book 1979; Teacher's Book, 1983.

28. Brown v. Board of Education of Topeca, 1954

The issue of segregation in schools has been one issue, if not the key one, in racial relations in the U.S.A.
The blacks could only hope for full recognition in American society and economic life when equality of educational opportunity was achieved.
In our context, the issue is of importance because it reveals the wavering stand of the Supreme Court - how, under public pressure, not least from the Civil Rights Movement, it finally reversed itself, thus proving its flexibility in the face of social changes.
Instead of quoting the reasonings of the Court at length, we chose those passages which reflect the major arguments of the Judges. Those who want to information on the full court proceedings will find them in:
Henry St. Commager **op.cit**, pp. 619-627 and in
Erwin Helms *America Today-Black America*, pp. 27-31

■ Additional text: Data on Blacks - Education, their Income, Unemployment Rates.

The latest available data from the year 1978 show that nationwide 38 per cent of black students were then attending schools with white majorities. The fact that progress was faster in the South (44%) than in the North (an estimated 28%) can be attributed partly to the concentration of the Northern black population in the depressed, ghetto-like central areas of large cities. (In 1980 58% of all American blacks lived in such areas). The physical separation of the races in major cities results in what is known as *de facto* segregation, in contrast to *de jure* (imposed by law) segregation, and makes an integration of public schools extremely difficult. Even the busing of black children to white schools and white children to black schools, ordered by the Supreme Court in 1970, has done little to improve the situation, not least because most parents, both white and black, prefer their children to attend schools in their own neighborhoods.
The advances made by the black population in the field of education as a result of the efforts of the Civil Rights Movement and of actions taken by Congress, the Supreme Court and U.S. Presidents are most clearly documented by the rise in the percentage of black children completing high school from 23 per cent in 1950 to 79 per cent in 1979. The situation is even more favorable in the field of higher education. According to the U.S. Bureau of Census Report of 1981, the number of blacks in colleges almost doubled between 1970 and 1980, so that at the end of the decade 28 per cent of all blacks between the ages of 18 and 24 were attending college.

It is obvious that it will take some time before these advances in educational standards will affect the economic situation of the blacks. If we compare the median incomes and unemployment rates of the black and white population, it becomes apparent that the blacks are still at a great disadvantage.

Median Family Income in 1982 and 1981 of all Families by Race

Region	1982			1981			Percent Change 1981-1982 (in current dollars)	
	Black	White	Black/ White	Black	White	Black/ White	Black	White
North East	14,735	25,815	.57	13,248	24,689	.54	4.8	-1.5
North Central	12,374	24,903	.50	14,837	23,886	.62	-21.4	-1.8
South	13,044	23,087	.56	12,283	22,051	.56	0.1	-1.3
West	16,508	25,249	.65	16,592	24,324	.68	-6.3	-2.2

Source: U.S. Department of Commerce, Census Bureau, Consumer Income, Series P-60, No. 140.

Unemployment Rates and Unemployment Ratios 1955-1983 for male workers by race

	18-19 years			20-24 years			25-34 years		
	Black	White	B/W Ratios	Black	White	B/W Ratios	Black	White	B/W Ratios
1955	12.9	10.4	1.2	12.4	7.0	1.8	8.6	2.7	3.2
1965	20.2	11.4	1.5	9.3	5.9	1.3	6.2	2.6	.2
1975	32.9	17.2	1.9	22.9	18.2	1.7	11.9	6.3	1.9
1982	47.4	21.1	2.2	32.0	15.3	2.1	19.6	10.4	1.9
1983	42.7	18.3	2.3	30.4	11.4	2.7	14.8	7.2	2.1

	35-44 years			45-54 years			55-64 years		
	Black	White	B/W Ratios	Black	White	B/W Ratios	Black	White	B/W Ratios
1955	8.2	2.7	3.2	6.4	2.9	2.2	9.0	3.9	2.3
1965	6.2	2.6	2.0	5.1	2.3	2.2	5.4	3.1	1.7
1975	11.9	6.3	1.9	9.0	4.4	.2	6.1	4.1	1.5
1982	19.6	10.4	1.9	10	6.3	1.6	11.9	5.8	.2
1983	14.8	7.2	2.1	12.1	4.6	2.6	7.3	4.7	1.5

If blacks today are less militant than they were in the fifties and sixties, then it is not only due to the fact that the gap between need expectation and fulfillment has become less intolerable, but also because they have learned to use the instrument of the vote: the percentage of blacks that register to vote today is almost equal to the percentage of whites registering. In many states and districts their vote has often become crucial. Using their vote, they have succeeded in placing black people in political office; the number of blacks holding political offices increased from fewer than 500 in 1965 to 5,160 in July, 1982. As the following table shows, more and more blacks have attained high-ranking positions:

	1972	1982
mayors	86	223 (1983: 236)
state legislators	169	347
House of Representatives	13	21
Senate	0	1

For up-to-date information and statistics on the Blacks consult: the *Annual Reports of the National Urban League*.

29. Eldridge Cleaver: Soul on Ice

Eldridge Cleaver was born in 1935; brought up in poverty and despair, he drifted early into petty crime and was sent to prison for trading marijuana. In 1966, together with Bobby Seale and Huey Newton, he founded the Black Panther Party (see text 30) and became its information minister and Presidential candidate (1968). After a shoot-out he was again sent to prison and after being charged with violating parole, convinced that he would not get a fair trial in the U.S.A., he fled to Cuba. From there he went to Algeria and visited a number of Communist countries including Soviet Russia, China, North Korea, and North Vietnam. From 1973 till his return to the U.S.A. in 1975, he lived in a working class district of Paris.

Cleaver's publications:
Soul on Ice, New York: McGraw Hill, 1968 (it sold more than 2 m copies in the U.S.A.)
Post-Prison Writings and Speeches. New York: Random House, 1970.

■ Additional Texts

Why I left the U.S. and Why I Am Returning.

I am often asked why I want to return to the United States...
I always take the opportunity to explain why I left in the first place. Lots of people believe I left because I preferred to go live in a Communist country, and that now, several years and many Communist countries later, I find the grass no greener on the Communist side of the fence. So now, here I stand, locked outside the gates of the paradise I once scorned, begging to be let back in. Let me clarify...

During the 1960's, the chips were down in a fateful way, uniting the upsurge of black Americans against the oppressive features of the system, and the gargantuan (huge) popular opposition to the Indochina wars...

A fabulous new era of progress is opening up to the world, and coping with all of the problems unleashed by Watergate has opened up a creative era for American democracy. I believe that every American, regardless of his politics, has a duty to re-examine some of his beliefs.

This is particularly true of those active at both extremes of the political spectrum. Those of us who developed a psychology of opposition must take a pause and sum up our experiences. We must recognize that in a sense we are playing in a brand new ball game. The slogans of yesterday will not get us through the tasks at hand. I believe that for America to deal with problems posed on the world level, a fundamental reorientation in the relationship between the American people is absolutely necessary.

With all of its faults, the American political system is the freest and most democratic in the world. The system needs to be improved, with democracy spread to all areas of life, particularly the economic. All of these changes must be conducted through our established institutions, and people with grievances must find political methods for obtaining redress.

Each generation subjects the world it inherits to severe criticism. I think that my generation has been more critical than most, and for good reason ... We should have discovered which values are worth conserving ... It is my hope to make a positive contribution in this regard.

Source: *New York Times, Nov. 18, 1975*

"How the prophet of violence became the apostle of brotherhood." (excerpts)

During his long exile, Cleaver experienced a radical change of heart, coming to the conclusion that his crude Marxism was untenable, that the United States, for all her faults, is and was the true home of liberty, and that the communist systems, which had once seemed to him to offer the hope of liberation for his race, threatened black and white with totalitarian despotism ...
It is clear that Mr. Cleaver's change of heart was, or more likely has now become, far more radical than that implied by his new-found political maturity. He has become a full and committed Christian ... What is more interesting in Mr. Cleaver's conversion is that he has not abandoned his belief that blacks in the United States are ill-used, cheated, discriminated against and unjustly treated; what he **has** abandoned is his former belief that violence is the way to change conditions. And now, as he faces both ways, he says:

"I don't know any other way of dealing with the past. You can't change it. You can't rewrite it. You can't suppress it or hide it. And you can't do it again. The best you can do is kind of learn from it ... So I criticize us for aiding, for importing ideologies."

(In the following passage Cleaver explains his present religious conviction and concludes:)

"I'm willing to say that I want to be a Christian. I want to believe in Jesus ... In the past I would just look at things as political or economic, without a moral or ethical dimension ... I see that that is the ultimate failure in dealing with human ... affairs. That the moment you throw out the moral and ethical considerations, you have reverted to the jungle."

Bernard Levin in *Times Newspaper*, 1977.

Either of these two texts or both may used in class for a test. **The students should be permitted to use a dictionary.**

Questions they should answer:

1. *Outline Cleaver's attitude before he left the U.S.A, and after he returned.*
2. *What has Cleaver in mind when he says "All of these changes must be conducted through our established institutions, and people with grievances must find political methods for obtaining redress?"*

30. <u>Program of the Black Panther Party</u>

Though the Black Panther Party as a consequence of systematic persecutions of its members by the police has practically been deprived of power, discussion of their program is of relevance to the objectives of this course, because

1. it gives a picture of the black discontent at its climax,
2. it reveals that even this extremely militant Afro-American organization refers to the Constitution as the mainstay of U.S. democracy.

For lack of space we were not able to reprint the Black Panther Party program with the comments its authors had attached to it. Since these comments in a number of points recur upon the Constitution, we reprint the full text here.

1. We want freedom. We want power to determine the destiny of our Black Community.

We believe that black people will not be free until we are able to determine our destiny.

2. We want full employment for our people.

We believe that the federal government is responsible and obligated to give every man employment or a guaranteed income. We believe that if the white American businessmen will not give full employment, then the means of production should be taken from the businessmen and placed in the community so that the people of the community can organize and employ all of its people and give a high standard of living.

3. We want an end to the robbery by the white man of our Black Community.

We believe that this racist government has robbed us and now we are demanding the overdue debt of forty acres and two mules. Forty acres and two mules was promised 100 years ago as restitution for slave labor and mass murder of black people. We will accept the payment in currency which will be distributed to our many communities. The Germans are now aiding the Jews in Israel for the genocide of the Jewish people. The Germans murdered six million Jews. The American racist has taken part in the slaughter of over fifty million black people; therefore, we feel that this is a modest demand that we make.

4. We want decent housing, fit for shelter of human beings.

We believe that if the white landlords will not give decent housing to our black community, then the housing and the land should be made into cooperatives so that our community, with government aid, can build and make decent housing for its people.

5. We want education for our people that exposes the true nature of this decadent American society. We want education that teaches us our true history and our role in the present-day society.

We believe in an educational system that will give to our people a knowledge of self. If a man does not have knowledge of himself and his position in society and the world, then he has little chance to relate to anything else.

6. We want all black men to be exempt from military service.

We believe that Black people should not be forced to fight in the military service to defend a racist government that does not protect us. We will not fight and kill other people of color in the world who, like black people, are being victimized by the white racist government of America. We will protect ourselves from the force and violence of the racist police and the racist military, by whatever means necessary.

7. We want an immediate end to POLICE BRUTALITY and MURDER of black people.

We believe we can end police brutality in our black community by organizing black self-defense groups that are dedicated to defending our

> *effect changes by stages* (Ed.'s italics). But to do all we want to do, we just have to go through all the stages of development. We cannot jump from A to Z as some thought ... It was arrogant of our party to criticize the Black community for not being ready to move as fast as we wanted them to.

31. <u>The Allan Bakke Case</u>

When President L.B. Johnson waged his "War Against Poverty," Congress, which then had a Democratic majority in both Houses, at Johnson's initiative passed a number of Civil Rights Laws which were meant to improve the situation of the disadvantaged and to guarantee equal opportunity for all.
In his own right, Johnson issued the **Executive Order 11, 246** (Sept. 16, 1965) on **Equal Employment Opportunity**, today generally referred to as **Affirmative Action.** Its goal was to promote the full realization of equal employment opportunity through *a positive continuing program* (Ed.'s italics) in each executive department and agency.

With this affirmative action, Johnson did not only intend to wipe out the effects of past discrimination, but also to improve the situation of the blacks and other disadvantaged groups employed by the government and those employed by contractors of the government. In case of their non-compliance, the administration threatened: "the contract may be cancelled, terminated, or suspended." In obeying this order many companies as well as some colleges and universities increased the number of disadvantaged and women on their staff or student body. But soon whites charged those who complied with this order with **reverse discrimination.** Our text outlines in detail why Bakke felt discriminated against and the reasoning of the Supreme Court. When the judges decided by a 5:4 vote that Bakke had to be admitted to the University of California, it emphasized that racial background may be used only under "certain conditions" in support of affirmative action; thus they reject the introduction of a **quota system**, i.e. basing admission to college on quotas related to the percentage of a given group of the population.

Students may discuss the pros and cons of such a quota system with reference to what we call 'Parteienproporz' in such institutions as a board of trustees (Rundfunkrat), a Court (Bundesverfassungsgericht) or equal representation of religious groups or women in public institutions, e.g. parties.

In the U.S.A., where in all fields of life, competition is an important factor, the quota system is highly controversial. Whilst the Blacks point to the demoralizing cycle of poverty and poor schooling, and consider this decision of the Supreme Court as the opening gambit in the Court's reversal of its earlier progressive position (e.g. Brown v. Board of Education of Topeca, see p. 62) and argue that objective test performance can have the effect of structuring socio-economic competition, whites are usually opposed to quota systems such as the preferential hiring of blacks.
That the attitude of the Supreme Court is ambivalent on this issue was revealed in a second case which it had to decide a year later. It then ruled (5:2) that a company did not violate Title VII of the **Civil Rights Act of 1964** when it tried

> to eliminate conspicuous racial imbalances in Kaiser's then almost exclusively white craftwork forces by reserving for black employees 50% of the openings in in-plant craft-training programs until the percentage of black craft workers in a plant is commensurate with the percentage of blacks in the local labor force.

See Helms, *America Today. Black America,* "United Steelworkers of America v. Brian F. Weber," pp. 45-46.

Lit. on Affirmative Action:
"Reverse Discrimination", in *Editorial Research Reports,* Aug.6, 1976.
James F. Scott "Brown and Bakke. The Relation between the Judicial Decision and Socioeconomic Conditions," in *Phylon,* Vol, XLI, No. 3, Sept. 1980.
R.A. Maidment "The US Supreme Court and Affirmative Action: The Cases of Bakke, Weber, and Fullilove," in *American Studies,* 15.3; pp. 34-356; CUP, 1981.

Today, powerful forces in the Reagan Administration, represented by Edwin Meese, Attorney General of the United States, are endeavoring to end affirmative action.
Have the students follow the issue in current publications.
Texts 29 and 30 supplied the students with information about individuals and groups who worked for the improvment of the socio-economic situation of the blacks at the grassroots. Their endeavours have not been in vain (see statistics on pp. 63-64).
To what extent the times have changed became apparent in 1984 when Jesse Jackson sought the presidential nomination of the Democratic Party. Never before had a black been as successful in the primary elections as he was: he received 18 per cent of the votes , as compared to Mondale's 39 and Hart's 36.

Jesse Jackson's speech, **Our Time Has Come**, delivered at the Democratic Convention in San Francisco in 1984, will give you an idea of how the most prominent black leader since Martin Luther King evaluates the American political situation today.

■ Additional text

Jesse Jackson

»Our Time Has Come«

Excerpts from the Speech to the Democratic Convention July 17, 1984*

Tonight we come together bound by our faith in a mighty God, with genuine respect and love for our country, and inheriting the legacy of a great party - a Democratic Party - which is the best hope for redirecting our nation on a more humane, just and peaceful course.

This is not a perfect party. We are not a perfect people. Yet, we are called to a perfect mission: our mission, to feed the hungry, to clothe the naked, to house the homeless, to teach the illiterate, to provide jobs for the jobless, and to choose the human race over the nuclear race.

We are gathered here this week to nominate a candidate and write a platform which will expand, unify, direct and inspire our party and the nation to fulfill this mission.

My constituency is the damned, disinherited, disrespected and the despised.

They are restless and seek relief. They've voted in record numbers. They have invested the faith, hope and trust that they have in us. The Democratic Party must send them a signal that we care. I pledge my best not to let them down.

There is the call of conscience: redemption, expansion, healing and unity. Leadership must heed the call of conscience, redemption, expansion, healing and unity, for they are the key to achieving our mission.

Time is neutral and does not change things.

[...]

America is a Quilt

Our flag is red, white and blue, but our nation is rainbow - red, yellow, brown, black and white - we're all precious in God's sight. America is not like a blanket - one piece of unbroken cloth, the same color, the same texture, the same size. America is more like a quilt - many patches, many pieces, many colors, many sizes, all woven and held together by a common thread.

The white, the Hispanic, the black, the Arab, the Jew, the woman, the Native American, the small farmer, the business-person, the environ-

*Reprinted from *Congressional Quarterly,* July 21, 1984, 1785-1789.

mentalist, the peace activist, the young, the old, the lesbian, the gay, and the disabled make up the American quilt.

Even in our fractured state, all of us count and fit somewhere. We have proven that we can survive without each other. But we have not proven that we can win or make progress without each other. We must come together.

From Fannie Lee Hamer in Atlantic City in 1964 to the Rainbow Coalition in San Francisco today; from the Atlantic to the Pacific, we have experienced pain but progress as we ended American apartheid laws; we got public accommodations; we secured voting rights; we obtained open housing;

I am more convinced than ever that we can win. We'll vault up the rough side of the mountain; we can win. I just want young America to do me one favor.

Exercise the right to dream. You must face reality - that which is. But then dream of the reality that ought to be, that must be. Live beyond the pain of reality with the dream of a bright tomorrow. Use hope and imagination as weapons of survival and progress. Use love to motivate you and obligate you to serve the human family.

Young America, dream. Choose the human race over the nuclear race. Bury the weapons and don't burn the people. Dream of a new value system. Teachers, who teach for life, and not just for a living, teach because they can't help it. Dream of lawyers more concerned with justice than a judgeship. Dream of doctors more concerned with public health than personal wealth. Dream *(sic)* preachers and priests who will prophesy and not just profiteer. Preach and dream. Our time has come.

Our time has come. Suffering breeds character. Character breeds faith. And in the end, faith will not disappoint.

Our time has come. Our faith, hope and dreams will prevail. Our time has come. Weeping has endured for the night. And, now joy cometh in the morning.

Our time has come. No graves can hold our body down.

Our time has come. No lie can live forever.

Our time has come. We must leave racial battleground and come to economic common ground and moral higher ground. America, our time has come.

We've come from disgrace to Amazing Grace, our time has come.

Give me your tired, give me your poor, your huddled masses who yearn to breathe free and come November, there will be a change because our time has come.

Thank you and God bless you.

Vocabulary:

inherit	receive as an heir, by birth
legacy	sth. handed down from ancestors
illiterate	unable to read and write
redemption	act of saving from evil
quilt	a thick bed-covering made up of patches of cloth
vault	an arched roof or ceiling, a cellar or subterranean storeroom

What was the purpose of this speech?
Collect some of his key words and describe what they reveal.
In putting together his "rainbow coalition" Jackson was careful to appeal to many disparate groups. Identify these groups. Why does he refer to "business-person" and not to "businessman"? The Reverend Jesse Jackson is a preacher. How is this reflected in his rhetoric?
Looking at his final passage you will notice that Jackson's main metaphor is that of the "dream". What use does he make of it?
To what extent does Jackson's rhetoric underline the urgency of his demands and hopes?
Sum up this chapter by outlining the changes in the Constitution, and the actions of the Executive, Legislative and Judicial branches of the government which helped to improve the situation of the blacks. Which measures do you think were the most effective?

The Constitution and Other Individual Rights. (Texts 32-40)

Of the rights guaranteed by the first ten Amendments of the Constitution, we have discussed freedom of religion at length.
The **right to bear arms** (Article 2) and **freedom of speech** throw additional light on the intentions of the Founding Fathers. Moreover, these rights have held a prominent position in recent discussions.

A "the right to bear arms"

The preliminary remarks in the Students' Book explain the historical reasons that led to the inclusion of this right in the Constitution, and also, why even in our time, it features so prominently in the minds of the Americans.
The validity of the statement made by Rap Brown, the leader of the Black Power Movement, that "Violence is as American as the Fourth of July and as cherry-pie," is borne out by history and confirmed by a look at American newspapers, radio and TV programs of our time.
In his contribution "Americanism" to
Dennis Welland (ed.) *The United States. A Companion to American Studies*, Prof. U.R. Brock of the University of Glasgow states:

> It can be argued that contemporary Americans are paying the price for a traditional tolerance of violence. It is frequently said that the Americans are a violent people, and this is stated as though it explains much. There has been a kind of perverse pride in the violence of the frontier ...
> The American tradition of violence is thus a convention rather than a historical truth, and the occasion on which it becomes real arose because people demanded too much and then refused to pay the price. Prohibition was a classic example: millions were asked suddenly to abandon a habit which they regarded as harmless and convivial, while a tiny handful of federal officers were employed at low salaries to enforce the law. Equally conducive to violence was the reluctance to meet nationwide crime with national police; criminal jurisdiction still remains in the hands of weak state governments ... (p. 83).

That Brock's comment, written with an eye on the race riots in the sixties and early seventies, still holds true, is borne out by recent Hollywood movies such as **Rocky** and **Rambo**, which **Newsweek** (Dec 23, 1985) describes as "twin icons of a flag waving, Red-baiting new Nationalism". The magazine also pointed out that "Psychologists (are) worried about the romanticized violence in both film cycles - the implicit message that the problems of 1985 can be solved in the manner of the frontier, by hitting or shooting guns ...".
If your students have seen one of these movies or both, you might discuss with them the validity of this statement and raise the question of whether the use of violence for a worthy end (trying to bring prisoners of war back from Vietnam) or just restoring pride in the U.S.A. can be justified.

For further information consult the report of a **Newsweek** team:

> Rocky and Rambo - Love him or hate him, with his two movie series, Sylvester Stallone has brought the hero back to the forefront of American mythology. (*Newsweek*, Dec. 12, 85)

In an earlier report (Oct.14,1985) *Newsweek* reported on "Machine Gun U.S.A. A flood of high-tech military weapons is raising the risks of criminal violence and testing the U.S. gun laws."
In this connection you should also make use of the advertisements in the Students' Book.

32. "If Guns Were Outlawed, Only Outlaws Would Have Guns"

The National Rifle Association (NRA) is one of the many lobbies that work in Washington D.C. and in the State capitals to influence policy-making decisions. NRA has 3 millions members. With its funds it has supported the election campaigns of many Congressmen, and now the chips are being called in relentlessly.
At present the pro-gun forces are supporting a reform of the **Gun Control Act of 1968** which had been passed by Congress after the assassinations of Robert F. Kennedy and Martin Luther King. The bill now being discussed is known as the **Firearm Owners Protection Bill**. If it is passed, it will be even easier to sell and buy guns. It also calls for less record-keeping and ends the system of surprise inspections of gun-dealers.
Mention should be made that there are also lobbies which oppose the Bill and demand a tightening of gun control such as **Handgun Control Inc.**
As hunting is a very popular sport in the U.S.A., it is easy to get a hunting licence; few people quarrel with sportsmen about their rifles, but they are worried about handguns, of which some 60 million are at present to be found in the U.S.A. Many people buy them for their protection, but they are also used for killing and robbing: nearly half of the 16,500 or so people murdered each year in the U.S.A. are killed with handguns (*The Economist*, March 8, 86)
A chart from *Scholastic Update* (Sept. 20, 1983) will give the students an idea of the frequency of crimes in the U.S.A. The question may be raised of whether any of these crimes might have been prevented if the victims had been armed.

Experts say that our fear of crime makes our crime problem seem worse than it is. Yet the numbers that define the problem provide little comfort. The U.S. suffered 22,000 murders last year.

33. The Subway Gunman
34. The Dangers of Self-Defense

A case which occurred before Christmas 1985 filled the columns of American newspapers and magazines for weeks and revived the discussion of the effectiveness of gun laws and of the right of an individual citizen to use violence in his or her self-defense.
Whilst the article from *Time* magazine describes the personality of Bernhard Hugo Goetz, his early experiences with assault, and the events that led to his shooting at four black teenagers, the excerpt from the *New York Times* comments on the problems involving self-defense.

After the students have acquainted themselves with the case and the questions it raises, have them answer a questionnaire used in a "Newsweek" poll. When they have answered the questions, inform them about the answers given by the Americans who participated in the poll.

As questions 6 and 9 involve the American scene only, you might leave them out or have the students answer them from their own perspective, i.e. have the events described happened to you in Germany and do you think that our police are able to protect you from violent crime?

After the students'answers have been collected, find the approval and disapproval rate and compare the result with the American figures. You might also use the comment by D.M. Alpern, esp. the last paragraph which gives information on the factors of race, sex, party affiliation and the environment's impact on the answers of the people polled.

■ Additional text:

A Newsweek Poll: 'Deadly Force'

Despite a 12-point rise in approval for Bernhard Goetz in the latest NEWSWEEK Poll—and the finding that three-quarters of those surveyed would also use deadly force for self-defense—an equally large majority believes that America's streets would actually be more dangerous if most people carried guns. Even a majority (56 percent) of those who carry or have carried guns agree.

The NEWSWEEK Poll found an increase in the number of people who said they kept a gun or weapon for protection, although previous Gallup surveys have shown little change in gun ownership. The difference may be that more people now view their weapons as means for self-defense. Those who said they actually *carried* guns or other weapons were mainly male and under 50 years of age. Only 7 percent of the women surveyed said they sometimes carried a gun or other weapon, but 24 percent of them said they have carried Mace, a whistle or some other defensive device. And among all the women and men who have been exposed to crime—as victims themselves or through the experience of relatives or friends—14 percent said they sometimes carried a weapon while 34 percent relied on defensive devices.

Of all those who approved of Goetz shooting four youths that he said threatened him in the New York subway, two-thirds felt he acted in self-defense. But about a third of Goetz's supporters felt he was acting more to get revenge for past brushes with crime and the justice system. Support for Goetz ran particularly high among men (62 percent), Republicans (63 percent), suburbanites (65 percent) and those who carry guns themselves (70 percent). Nonwhites divide almost evenly on the case, with 39 percent approving the Goetz shootings and 43 percent disapproving. But a solid majority of nonwhites (56 percent) agreed with the white majority that race was not a significant factor in the incident.

DAVID M. ALPERN

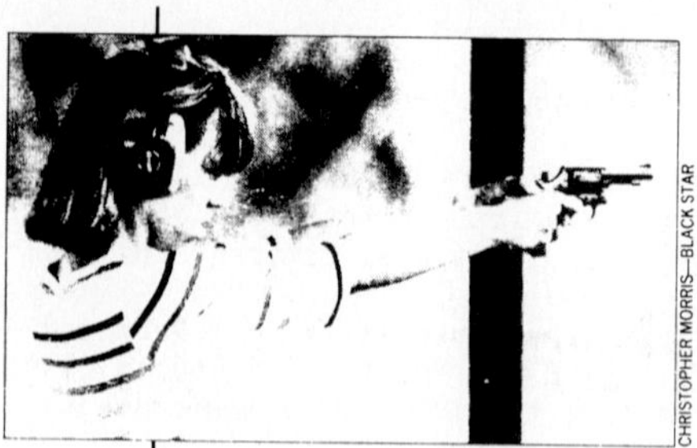

CHRISTOPHER MORRIS—BLACK STAR

From what you know about the Goetz case so far, do you tend to approve or disapprove of Goetz shooting four youths on a New York subway?*

	3/85	1/85 ABC
Approve	**57%**	**45%**
Disapprove	**28%**	**46%**
Don't know	**15%**	**9%**

From what you know about the case, do you feel Goetz shot the youths *more* out of fear for his own life at the moment, OR *more* to get revenge for past muggings and the failings of the justice system?*

More out of fear for his life	**53%**
More to get revenge	**29%**

Do you think the fact that Goetz was white and the youths were black was a significant factor in causing him to shoot them or not?*

Yes 19% **No 70%** **Don't know 11%**

Do you feel that taking the law into one's own hands, often called vigilantism, is justified by circumstances?

	3/85	2/14/85 Gallup
Always	**3%**	**8%**
Sometimes	**68%**	**72%**
Never	**23%**	**17%**

If the situation arose, would you use deadly force against another person in self-defense?

Yes 78% **No 13%** **Don't know 9%**

Please tell me if any of the following have happened to you in the past 12 months:

	3/85	1/81
Assaulted or mugged	**2%**	**3%**
House broken into	**19%**	**14%**
Heard a friend was assaulted/mugged	**25%**	**—**

Which of the following steps do you take or have you taken to deal with crime?

	3/85	1/81
Keep a gun or other weapon	**46%**	**31%**
Try not to go out alone at night	**54%**	**64%**
Avoid certain areas even during the day	**43%**	**60%**
Carry a gun or other weapon	**10%**	**—**
Carry a defensive device such as Mace, a whistle or alarm	**17%**	**—**

If most people carried guns, do you think the streets would be safer or more dangerous?

Safer 11% **More dangerous 78%**
No difference 3% **Don't know 8%**

How much confidence do you have in the ability of the police to protect you from violent crime?

	3/85	1/81
Great deal	**15%**	**15%**
Quite a bit	**37%**	**34%**
Not very much	**39%**	**42%**
None at all	**6%**	**8%**
Don't know	**3%**	**1%**

Do you think the Goetz incident has made people more willing to physically resist criminals or not?

Yes 55% **No 24%** **Don't know 21%**

*Asked of the 87% of those interviewed who said they had read or heard about the case.
For this NEWSWEEK Poll, The Gallup Organization interviewed 1,009 adults by telephone on Feb. 28 and March 1. The margin of error is plus or minus 4 percentage points. Some "Don't know" responses omitted. The NEWSWEEK Poll © 1985 NEWSWEEK, Inc.

CORNELIS VAN DEN HEUVEL—NEWSWEEK

Newsweek,
March 11,1985

If you want to go beyond the American scene, you may discuss with your students such questions as

1. If peaceful means of dissent fail, is violence justified?

2. Does dissent become something else when it is accompanied by violence? Explain your reasoning.

A quotation from A.M. Schlesinger, *Jr. Ideas, Power and Violence in America*, Boston: Houghton Mifflin, 1969, may be used as basis for a discussion:

> A limited amount of collective violence may stimulate the process of democratic change; but, if the left, through the cult of the deed, helps create an atmosphere which destroys the process of democracy itself, the only winners will be those who use violence best, and they will be on the right. (p. 34)

For further information:

Jack Zevin (ed.) *Violence in America: What Is the Alternative?* Englewood Cliffs, N.J. Prentice Hall, 2nd ed. 1973.
(This is one of a collection of texts *Inquiry Into Crucial American Problems* which is used in many American schools).
Arthur A. Ekirch, Jr. (ed.) *Voice of Dissent. An Anthology of Individual Thought in the U.S.*, New York: Citadel Press, 1964. (Signet Book 1963)
Fictional prose: Truman Capote *In Cold Blood*, New York: Random House, 1965.
Claude Brown: *Manchild in the Promised Land*. New York: MacMillan, 1965.
Louise Y. Gosset *Violence in Recent Southern Fiction*. Durham, N.C., Duke

University Press, 1965.
(Deals with Wolfe, Caldwell, Faulkner, Styron, Capote, and others)

■ Additional text (suitable for a written test):

Let Us Now Praise Anger

OPINION/GEORGE F. WILL

[...]

Many New Yorkers are angry because they believe justice is a rare accident. They believe that few violent criminals are caught, that many fewer are convicted, that most of those convicted plea-bargain their way to leniency. That is true. In 1983 in the city there were 84,043 reported robberies. There were just 7,351 convictions, all but 663 by plea-bargaining. There were 26,808 reported felonious assaults, just 727 convictions, all but 61 by plea-bargaining. Persons dependent on the subway—a nightmare of spray-painted graffiti that underscores the menacing environment of lawlessness—can become desperate.

Let us now praise anger, and especially anger in the form of a desire for justifiable vengeance. Ours is an age that overvalues the "well-adjusted" person without inquiring as to the nature of the circumstances to which we are supposed to adjust ourselves. (A well-adjusted subway rider would worry me.) We have been plied and belabored with the notion that anger is invariably a dysfunction, a "failure to cope" with our "environment." Great literature from Homer on (Nicholas Nickleby was splendidly angry) teaches otherwise; it teaches that anger can be necessary for coping. We are told that a desire for vengeance is primitive and shameful. But Hamlet's desire was noble.

Enemies of Serenity: When a society becomes, like ours, uneasy about calling prisons penitentiaries or penal institutions, and instead calls them "correctional institutions," the society has lost its bearings. If prisoners are "corrected," that is nice but it is an ancillary outcome. The point of imprisonment is punishment. The idea of punishment is unintelligible if severed from the idea of retribution, which is inseparable from the concept of vengeance, which is an expression of anger. No anger, no justice. A society incapable of sustained, focused anger in the form of controlled vengeance is decadent. What the man did in the subway pleased the community because it satisfied a desire for vengeance against the enemies of serenity. The community's pleasure, although not thought through (and perhaps only because it is not thought through) is wholesome.

If we lived in a world in which vengeance really was "senseless," so would life be. Life would be, as Macbeth said, "a tale told by an idiot." But "Macbeth" is about justified anger producing virtuous vengeance. If you will not take Shakespeare's word for it, take Clint Eastwood's—or else. Because of the "Dirty Harry" movies, Eastwood is a megastar. [...]

The movies express an idea that is debatable (that liberal court rulings have unjustly helped criminals). But the movies satisfy a longing we should want to keep strong—a longing for justice. It is healthy anger that causes New Yorkers to take pleasure from what the man did in the subway and it is not obvious that what he did was unhealthy.

Excerpt from *Newsweek*, Jan.14, 1985.

plea bargain	talk of an agreement to settle a case usually by admitting that the defendant is guilty
leniency	merciful judgment
felonious	from 'felony'= a serious crime
be plied with	to be urged, worked upon
cope with	deal successfully with
penitentiary	from penitence (dt. Reue): prison
ancillary	additional
retribution	deserved punishment
serenity	tranquillity, calm peace

Comment on Will's statements:

"No anger, no justice."
"It is healthy anger that causes New Yorkers to take pleasure from what the man did in the subway and it is not obvious that what he did was unhealthy."

B Freedom of Speech and of the Press

Whilst the "right to bear arms" must be considered as a controversial issue among Americans, the freedom of speech and of the press will be defended by almost all Americans.
The texts we present deal with cases in which interested groups appealed to the Supreme Court to uphold this right. Americans who discuss these freedoms usually do not only refer to the First Amendment but also to the Tenth which runs:

> The powers not delegated by the Constitution to the United States, nor prohibited by it to the States, are reserved to the States respectively, or *to the people* (Ed.'s italics).

The doctrine of free speech and of the press is based on the free competition of opinion in the open market; which means that every citizen must be permitted to express his own opinion freely.
The Connecticut Constitution of 1818 said: "Every citizen may speak, write, and publish his sentiments on all subjects, being responsible for the abuse of that liberty."
Cases that deal with these freedoms therefore mostly have to do with such abuses or alleged abuses. They involve such questions as: "Is it legitimate to deny these rights to those whose avowed aim is to destroy democratic government?" "Can these rights be denied to those who use free speech to serve their own interests by supposedly distorting the truth (the **Near** case) or betraying the public interest (President Nixon - Watergate)?"

If one of your students wants to become a journalist, he or she could be asked to report on the **Federal Freedom of Information Act.**

■ Additional text:

Freedom of Information Act

Signed into law in 1966, took effect in 1967. It provided that citizens could request access to government records, documents and papers and, if they were not forthcoming, file suit in federal court to obtain them. Exemptions were provided in several categories. Among the exemptions were national security information, trade or financial secrets, personnel and medical files and correspondence between officials. Public access to government documents had previously been determined by a broad "need to know" policy. The Administrative Procedure Act of 1946 contained a general provision for public disclosure but added that documents could be withheld "for good cause found" or "in the public interests."

The Freedom of Information Act itself was found to work inefficiently. A House subcommittee concluded after hearings in 1972 that its operation had been "hindered by five years of foot-dragging by the federal bureaucracy." Seventeen amendments to the law were passed in 1974 over President Gerald Ford's veto; Ford said the measure was a threat to U.S. "military or intelligence secrets and diplomatic relations." The amendments gave easier access to information, required a "reasonable" description rather than an exact description of the document being sought, set a 10-day limit for response to requests for data and a 20-day limit for rulings on appeals. Courts could inspect classified documents and review the justification for their classification; the burden of proof was on the government to justify a secrecy classification.

About 150,000 requests for information were presented to government agencies under the liberalized law in 1976. The Justice Department processed 51,000 requests, the Defense Department, almost 44,000. Of the total number of requests, 24,600 were denied. Appeals were made in 4,200 cases, and some 3,700 appeals were decided that year. In 12 percent of the appeals, the government agency reversed itself; in 42 percent, part of the information was released; in 46 percent, the denial was sustained.

Great quantities of material have been obtained under the act, and worthwhile results achieved. For example, the Central Intelligence Agency "was forced to reveal its top-secret MK-Ultra program of drug experimentation on humans," Time reported. "Ralph Nader used the act to pry out documents for his successful campaign against carcinogenic Red Dye No. 2." Thousands of pages of documents on the case of Julius and Ethel Rosenberg and the assassinations of John F. Kennedy and Martin Luther King were released, others noted.

Appraisals of the extent to which the press had used - or been able to use - the legisation varied. The act's exemptions were left largely intact, and some agencies "still invoke them extravagantly," Newsweek commented. More than three out of every five requests for information are filed not by scholars, Representatives, public-interest advocates or journalists, Allen Weinstein wrote in the New York Times, but by the business community and the law firms representing it. A Washington radio newsman contended, "It's a tremendous weapon, and one that reporters are going to have to learn to use."

In a test of the law in 1979, the Supreme Court ruled unanimously that private parties did not have the right to use the Freedom of Information Act to prevent government disclosure of information. A growing number of companies had filed so-called "reverse Freedom of Information suits" to block the release of material they had supplied to the government. The High Court held that the information act was "purely a disclosure statute," protecting "the submitters' interest in confidentiality only to the extent that this interest is endorsed by the agency collecting the information."

The Supreme Court narrowed the scope of the Freedom of Information Act in two 1980 cases. It ruled 5-2 that government agencies were not obligated under the act to retrieve documents that had been removed from their possesssion. Justice William H. Rehnquist wrote in the majority opinion that a federal agency could not be accused of improperly withholding a document if it had been removed prior to the request for it. "In such cases, the agency has neither the custody or control necessary to enable it to withhold," Rehnquist said. The ruling was made in Kissinger v. Reporters Commitee for Freedom of the Press.

The High Court ruled 7-2 in the second case, Forsham v. Harris, that private organizations receiving federal funds were not required to turn over data requested under the act. Rehnquist, again writing for the majority, held that such data did not qualify as "agency records" within the terms of the act.

Soon after the Reagan administration took office in 1981, Attorney General William French Smith announced a new policy for releasing government documents. Smith put the Justice Department on call to defend all suits brought against an agency for denial of information under the Freedom of Information Act. The suit would not be pursued only if it was determined that the legal basis was not adequate for defense or that a defense could adversely affect the ability of other agencies to protect records. Later that year, William J. Casey, director of the Central Intelligence Agency, urged that intelligence agencies be granted "total exclusion" from the requirements of the information act. And the administration sent to Congress proposals to curb the act's provisions for release of information. The administration sought authority for the attorney general to decide the categories of information to be withheld, subject to court appeal.

In 1982, the Senate Judiciary Committee voted 15-0 to leave the Freedom of Information Act substantially as it was. The committee rejected administration proposals to weaken the law. Meanwhile, the Supreme Court ruled unanimously that citizenship data was not subject to automatic disclosure under the act, that courts must decide whether release of the information would constitute an unwarranted invasion of personal privacy. The case was U.S. v. Washington Post.

Paneth, Donald. <u>Encyclopedia of American Journalism, Facts on File</u>, 1983

Further information in:
Christine M. Marwick *Your Right to Government Information*, New York: Bantam Books, 1985; pp. 217-225.
Commission of Freedom of the Press: *A Free and Responsible Press, a general report on mass communication: newspapers, radio, motion pictures, magazines and books.* Chicago University Press, 1947.

37. Near v. Minnesota

This outline of the **Near v. Minnesota** case which dispenses with the lengthy court arguments will enable the students
1. to study the application of the First Amendment to a practical case;
2. to discuss the problems of censorship by the government;
3. to understand the functioning of the U.S. legal system;
4. to point out the effect of precedents on future court decisions (see text 39); and
5. to make the acquaintance of the structure of the legal system and to the language of law.

ad 1.
The **Public Nuisance Law of 1925** of the State of Minnesota permitted a single judge acting without a jury to stop the publication of a newspaper or magazine, if it published "obscene, lewd, and lascivious ... or malicious, scandalous, and defamatory" matter (that's why it was called a "gag law".)
In the twenties, after Prohibition had been introduced with the 18th Amendment in 1920, (repealed with the 21th Amendment in 1933), Minneapolis had become a crossroads in the illegal liquor trade. The city was being run by corrupt politicians and gangsters. Besides gambling and illegal booze, there were numerous killings. Whilst the respectable newpapers refused to investigate the association between the law-breakers and the law enforcement officers, Near, with his *Saturday Press*, reported such scandals. Among the officials was the county prosecutor. Near claimed that he was dragging his feet in the investigation of gangland pursuits. Thereupon the prosecutor filed a complaint under the Public Nuisance Law.

ad 2.
The discussion should hinge on whether the government authorities have the right of **prior restraint**, i.e. to prohibit a newspaper from publishing materials of which they disapprove or to interfere only after a newspaper has published scandalous and possibly untrue material.
It should be pointed out that the U.S. Constitution is vague in this respect (the reason why this case ultimately came before the U.S. Supreme Court), whilst the German Grundgesetz in Article 5 apart from guaranteeing the freedom of speech and of the press states clearly: "Eine Zensur findet nicht statt."
In this context the students may be asked whether at a time when movies and TV uninhibitedly present cases of brutality and when pornographic material is easily available, the issue of "prior restraint" ought to be reconsidered. What are the implications of "prior restraint" upon a newspaper run by students?

ad 3.
A close study of the text reveals that the Near case was first tried by a county court, then by the Supreme Court of Minnesota. Both courts upheld the temporary restraining order. As Near and McCormick wanted to prevent the order from becoming **permanent**, they went through the same procedure a second time, because only after the Minnesota Supreme Court had rejected their appeal could Near, supported by McCormick, take the case to the U.S. Supreme Court (this explains why the case took four years).

In this connection it is necessary to know that the U.S. Supreme Court only reviews cases which involve the most basic constitutional questions affecting the whole nation.
Of some 5000 requests that arrive at the Supreme Court each year, it accepts about 450, and less than 200 of these cases receive a full hearing.

ad 4.
In 1971, the Supreme Court relied on the "Near" precedent in the Pentagon Papers case (see text 38.)

ad 5.

The structure	**the officers**	**terminology**
county courts	county judge	prior restraint restraining order
state Supreme Courts	county prosecutor	to claim to reject a claim
US Supreme Court	Supr.C. judge or justice	arguments for and against the case to argue a case
(to relieve the SC, 91 US District Courts and 11 US Courts have been created (see Article III of the Constitution),	attorney	hearings appeal injunction (einstweilige Verfügung) defendant charge to commit an offense libel laws

Lit. *Guide to the Supreme Court*. Washington D.C.: Quarterly Incorp., 1979.
Helms *U.S.A. - Staat und Gesellschaft* "Die richterliche Gewalt" pp. 86-96.

38. Ellsberg and the Pentagon Papers

Successive Presidents (John F. Kennedy, Lyndon B. Johnson, and Richard M. Nixon) were involved in the Vietnam War (1962-1975). In 1967, Robert S. McNamara, who was then Secretary of Defense, commissioned a massive top-secret history of the U.S. role in the Indochina War which became known as the Pentagon Papers.
This short interview illustrates how the Pentagon Papers got into the hands of David Ellsberg. It explains why Ellsberg changed from "hawk" to "superdove", and how the New York Times obtained most of the narrative history and documents.
Additional explanations: the **Rand Corporation**, like the Brookings Institution, the American Enterprise Institute, the Hoover Institute and the Heritage Institute is one of the many "think tanks" that supply influential political circles with information.

Lit. Donald T. Chritchlow *The Brookings Institution 1916-52. Expertise and the Public Interest in a Democratic Society,* Northern Illinois University, 1986.

39. <u>U.S. Government v. New York Times and Washington Post, 1971</u>

After the first three daily instalments of the Pentagon Papers had appeared, the Justice Department obtained a **temporary** restraining order (see text 37). The Government, contending that if public dissemination of the history continued "the national defense interests of the United States and the nation's security will suffer immediate and irreparable harm," argued for a **permanent** injunction.
When the case came before the U.S. Supreme Court, the judges ruled 6:3 against the Government.
Discussing Justice Black's opinion, it should be pointed out:

1. that he based his opinion on the First Amendment,as the Court had done in the Near-case.
2. that he came out fully in support of a free and unrestrained press.
3. that he included in his opinion an almost emotional statement ("... the duty of the press to prevent the Government from sending people off to distant lands to die of foreign wars and foreign shot and shell").
4. that he ends up with a moral judgment: the NYT and the Washington Post "should be commended"; they "nobly did precisely that which the founders hoped and trusted they would do."

40. <u>The Watergate Scandal</u>

In the Ellsberg interview it was already mentioned that a spy ring operation from the White House had broken into the office of Ellsberg's psychiatrist. These **plumbers** were the same who broke into the Headquarters of the Democratic Party in the Watergate building in Washington, D.C.
This text is of special interest to non-American teachers, because it is taken from a U.S. school text-book prepared by American teachers.

Additional information:

New Frontier - J.F. Kennedy's program outlined in his Nomination Acceptance speech at the Democratic National Convention on July 15, 1960. (Full text in Hildegard Gauger/Hermann Metzger *J.F. Kennedy Speaks* Tübingen: Max Niemeyer, 1964).

Great Society - L.B. Johnson's program outlined in a speech delivered on May 22, 1964.
During Johnson's presidency such important acts as the Civil Rights Acts (1964), the Economic Opportunity Act (1964), the Voting Rights Act (1965) and various Education Acts were passed by Congress.
<u>Lit.</u> Doris Kearns *Lyndon Johnson and the American Dream.* New York: Harper & Row, 1976.

Oil crisis - 1973.
- To curtail the consumption of gasoline, Congress limited the maximum speed on all American roads and highways to 55 m.p.h.

Paris talks - started in 1969, but soon deadlocked, when Nixon offered peace proposals which required the Communists to silence their guns and to allow free elections in South Vietnam; they were rejected by the Communists.

It should be pointed out to the students that during those years the original trust of the American people in their government (73% in 1960) had changed into increasing distrust (68% in 1980). This decline is to a large extent explained by the effect the publication of the Pentagon Papers and the Watergate affair had upon the Americans.
Ronald Reagan succeeded in restoring trust, at least in the President: in

1986 85% approved his handling of American affairs. It declined again after the Iran-Contra affair in 1986.

Lit.:
Lewis Chester et al. *Watergate. The Full Inside Story* New York: Ballantine Books, 1973.

When the cases presented in this section on the freedom of speech and of the press have been analysed and discussed, the students should connect the insights gained with the principles involved.
A passage from Walter Lippmann *The Public Philosophy*, 1955, may be used for this purpose.
Walter Lippman, American essayist and editor, was born in New York in 1889. After graduating from Harvard, he became editor of mostly liberal newspapers, and later highly respected for his syndicated columns. He died in 1974.
Book publications; *A Preface to Politics* (1913), *Public Opinion* (1922), *A Preface to Morals* (1929).

■ Additional text:

DEBATE AS THE ESSENTIAL PRINCIPLE OF FREEDOM OF SPEECH

by *W. Lippmann*

Nobody can justify in principle, much less in practice, a claim that there exists an unrestricted right of anyone to utter anything he likes at any time he chooses. There can, for example, be no right, as Mr. Justice Holmes said, to cry "Fire!" in a crowded theatre. Nor is there a right to tell a customer that the glass beads are diamonds, or a voter that the opposition candidate for President is a Soviet agent.

Freedom of speech has become a central concern of the western society because of the discovery among the Greeks that dialectic, as demonstrated in the Socratic dialogues, is a principal method of attaining moral and political truth. The right to speek freely is one of the necessary means to the attainment of the truth. That, and not the subjective pleasure of utterance, is why freedom is a necessity in the good society. Freedom of speech is conceived as the means to a confrontation of opinion. And because the purpose of the confrontation is to discern truth, there are rules of evidence and of parliamentary procedure, there are codes of fair dealing and fair comment, by which a loyal man will consider himself bound when he exercises the right to publish opinions. For the right to freedom of speech is no license to deceive, and willful misrepresentation is a violation of its principles.

In our time the application of these fundamental principles poses many unsolved practical problems. For the modern media of mass communication do not lend themselves easily to a confrontation of opinions. The dialectical process for finding truth works best when the same audience hears all the sides of the disputation. This is manifestly impossible in the moving pictures: if a film advocates a thesis, the same audience cannot be shown another film designed to answer it. Radio and television broadcasts do permit some debate. But despite the effort of the companies to let opposing views be heard equally, and to organize programs on which there are opposing speakers, the technical conditions of broadcasting do not favor genuine and productive debate. For the audience, tuning on and tuning off here and there, cannot be counted upon to hear, even in summary form, the essential evidence and the main arguments on all the significant sides of a question. Rarely, and on very few public issues, does the mass audience have the benefit of the process by which truth is sifted from error: the dialectic of debate in which there are immediate challenge, reply, cross-examination, and rebuttal. The men who regularly broadcast the news and comment upon the news cannot — like a speaker in the Senate or in the House of Commons — be challenged by one of their listeners and compelled then and there to verify their statements of fact and to re-argue their inferences from the facts.

Yet, when genuine debate is lacking, freedom of speech does not work as it is meant to work. It has lost the principle which regulates it and justifies it — that is to say, dialectic conducted according to logic and the rules of evidence. If there is no effective debate, the unresticted right to speak will unloose so many propagandists, procurers, and panderers upon the public that sooner or later in self-defense the people will turn to the censors to protect them. For, in the absence of debate, unrestricted utterance leads to the degradation of opinion. The opinions that will prevail will be those which are held most ardently by those with the most passionate will. For that reason the freedom to speak can be maintained only by promoting debate. In the end, what men will most ardently desire is to suppress those who disagree with them and, therefore, stand in the way of the realization of their desires. Thus, once confrontation in debate is no longer necessary, the toleration of all opinions leads to intolerance. Freedom of speech, separated from its essential principle, leads through a short transitional chaos to the destruction of freedom of speech.

Vocabulary :

sift	separate, pass through a sieve (dt. Sieb)
rebuttal	overthrowing by contrary evidence
inference	the meaning one draws from sth. done or said
panderer	dt. Verführer
procurer	dt. Kuppler
degradation	reduction in estimation
transitional	passing from one condition to another

Discuss the necessity of free speech and the dangers involved in it.

Lit.

Paul L. Murphy *The Meaning of Freedom of Speech.* Westport, CO.: Greenwood Press, 1972

Doris A. Graber *Media Power in Politics.* Washington, D.C. Congressional Quarterly, 1984

Of other rights enumerated in the **Bill of Rights** those outlined in the **8th Amendment** have recently been in the forefront in the discussion about the death penalty. Those opposing the death penalty refer to the clause "nor (shall) cruel and unusual punishment be inflicted." Whilst in 1972 the Supreme Court had declared the death penalty unconstitutional, it reversed its stand in 1976 and ruled in a 7:2 decision that the death penalty did not violate the Eighth Amendment, arguing that a number of states had legalized it. It considered this an indication that society approved of it:

> We hold that the death penalty is not a form of punishment that may never be imposed regardless of the character of the offender and regardless of the procedure followed in reaching the decision to impose it.

Today 39 states impose it.
Again proof of the flexibility of the U.S. political system!

■ Mention might also be made of the **Fourth Amendment**, because it touches upon a problem that is at present of great concern to young Americans. It relates directly to the increasing violence which is often caused by the drug addiction

of young people.
The gist of the Fourth Amendment is: "The right of the people to be secure in their persons, houses, papers, and affects, *against unreasonable searches and seizures* (Ed.'s italics), shall not be violated."
The excerpt from a TV series *The Law Works,* aired in 1982, reprinted in the Students' magazine *Senior Scholastic* of April 30, 1982, is based on a true story.
A high school student, Nate, buys marijuana from another student. The school janitor observes the transaction and reports it to the principal, Miss Clarkson, who then allows the narcotics officer to search the student's locker. Marijuana is found. Miss Clarkson justifies her action, reasoning that as the principal of the school she is empowered by the community to take care of their children whenever the school is open.
After these facts have been presented to the studio audience, the following discussion ensues, guided by Prof. Arthur Miller of the Harvard Law School:

Miller: Now listen, listen. Let's see where we are in this discussion. What Miss Clarkson is saying to you is that she's not controlled by the Fourth Amendment. That she's acting the way your parents would act during school hours and she has her own standards for controlling the safety and educational process of the school. And what she is saying to you is that, in her judgment, she thinks that there is a drug problem. She believes she has the right to search lockers to get drugs out of the school. Let's remember something from the film. In the film, both Miss Clarkson and the detective were involved in that search. Now, how did the detective get into your locker? Did he have a warrant?
Nate . . .?

Nate: She let him in.

Miller: Didn't he have a warrant?

Nate: No.

Miller: But I thought the police required a warrant and a probable cause. (*To Clarkson*:) How did you let the cop in?

Nate: That's what I'd like to know.

Clarkson: I did believe what the janitor said . . . . I wanted to go down there and look into that locker. Because the policeman was with me, I gave him permission to go into the locker.

Miller: Miss Clarkson has just told us that she gave away Nate's protection against the police.

David: What gives you the right to give the policeman rights? He can violate anyone's rights if you say so?

Miller: Carl has just given you the answer. She has the right to go into the locker, so she is just passing it along to the police.

Teenager: What gives her the right to pass it along?

Miller: O.K. Let's see where we are. We've seen Miss Clarkson is not controlled by the Fourth Amendment: She doesn't need probable cause. She doesn't need a search warrant. She's got a school to take care of. And during school hours, at least, the law or society has made the judgement that she is like your parents. She can even give the right to look into your locker to the police even though the police would have needed a warrant to come in on their own.
Now, let's go back to your house.
You are at home now and the

police have come to search your room for drugs. But they don't have a warrant. Now we've already learned that you don't have to let them in. But it's your parents who have answered the door. And they said, "Sure, go ahead, if he is smoking pot he has got to be taught a lesson." Now your bedroom is your most private area. It is far more private than your locker. So do you think that the parents can consent to giving away your Fourth Amendment rights? What do you think, Gary?

Gary: Well I think that they can. My parents, I don't think, would do that. I mean, I think we have an understanding and they would come to me.

Miller: You say that the Fourth Amendment doesn't protect you against your parents giving the cops the right to come in?

Gary: It doesn't really. But I think we have the relations, the understanding.

Miller: But you're admitting that they can give it away just the way Miss Clarkson in a sense, gave it away.

Teenager: I think your parents should confront you just like the principal should confront you before they take any action.

Teenager: What you are saying is that as long as your parents are there, if you are under 18, you've got no Fourth Amendment rights at all.

Miller: You're walking on the street. The police can't stop you. What we are really saying is that you are covered by this thing called the Fourth Amendment and we are carving out little areas (exceptions.) One is your parents at home. One is your principal at school.

Teenager: So you've got no rights at home for Fourth Amendment and no rights at school for Fourth Amendment.

Miller: We've learned a great deal about your privacy rights today. Now generally, the police need two things to search your private places. First, a good reason—what the law calls *probable cause*. And second, a search warrant. But principals and parents don't need either one and they may be able to let police into spaces where the police couldn't search if they were acting alone without a warrant. Because parents and principals can search you and your things and can even consent to police searches, you actually have less Fourth Amendment protection against parents and principals than against the police. And it is understandable that you might feel deprived of your rights.

Now the theory is that parents and educators are responsible for raising good citizens. And the law wants these people to know when your activities are questionable. So they can help straighten you out and prevent you from becoming a problem as an adult. This duty is simply deemed more important than your right to privacy. And so parents and principals have the authority to search.

But just because other people have legal control over you, and that's what we have been talking about, you do really have some protection. Remember, your principal and your parents have your best interests at heart. They'll try to protect you. And it is a relationship so if you act responsibly toward them and the law maybe you really don't have anything to worry about. So thanks for joining us on *The Law Works.* □

This text again offers an opportunity of role-play.

ERIC ROTH

Going through Nate's locker, the detective finds marijuana in Nate's jacket.

ERIC ROTH

Called to the principal's office, Nate is searched by a detective.

Questions

1. What would have happened in a German school?

2. Are German citizens protected against search and seizure?

Basic Principles (Texts 41-44)

Introductory comment

Whilst in the previous chapters we deliberately abstained from analyzing the Constitution directly, but offered instead case studies of the past and present that bear on the US Constitution, this chapter attempts to clarify a number of the basic concepts:

federalism,
government by checks and balances,
the division of powers, and
government based on the consent of the governed.

A. Federalism

The preliminary remarks, in the Students' Book give a rough outline of the development of Federalism in the U.S.A.
To illustrate how powers are divided between the Federal and the State governments, use the table on p. 115 of the Students'Book.
Have two students give a summary of the regulations of the Constitution set down in Articles 1, ,8, 9, and 10, and let all students look closely at the 10th Amendment.
Then have them list from the previous texts examples that show what use the Federal Government made of the powers invested in it (texts 5, 22-24, 27, 29, and 34).
You might refer to some other examples, e.g.

1. *the Tennessee Valley Authority, which in the thirties regulated the building of hydro-electric power dams.*
   The TVA Act of 1933 launched the Federal Government into a vast scheme of regional planning;
   Lit. D.E. Lilienthal *TVA-Democracy on the March.* rev.ed. 1953.
2. *the 55 mile per hour regulation, the speed limit which was introduced after the oil crisis in 1973;*
3. *the building of interstate highways.*

As an example of the states refusing to comply with a suggestion from Congress, you should refer to their refusal to accept the Equal Rights Amendment (text 22).
If you want your students to compare US Federalism with our `Bundestaat'(again an opportunity for 'fächerübergreifendes Arbeiten'), you may consult:
Informationen zur Politischen Bildung, Heft 169, "Föderalismus - die BRD als Bundesstaat." Bonn: Bundeszentrale für politische Bildung, 1976, or make use of the **Grundgesetz**, Art. 20, 25, and 29. Other relevant articles of the GG are 31, 32, 37, 70-75, and 105, which stress the rights of the Federal Government; and Articles 30, 50-53, and 83-85, which deal with the rights of the 'Bundesländer'.
As an additional question, you may ask the students to name nations that are organized as ***federal*** *or* ***unitary*** *states, and then discuss the pros and cons of* ***centralization*** *and* ***decentralization*** *(e.g. centralization may prevent duplication of effort; decentralization allows more "Bürgernähe"), also what impact the historical development of each country, its size and the character of its population have had on the structuring of these nations.*

Lit.
U.S. Constitution, Amendments 10, 14, and 17, (see Appendix)
Paul D. Fogel "American Federalism." In: *American Studies Newsletter.* Bonn: US Embassy, USIA, 1982.

"Federalism in the U.S.A." In: *American Studies Newsletter,* Bonn, USIA, 1985.
Daniel J. Elazar "Federalism in America." In: *Dialogue*, No 58, 4/1982.
Hamilton/Madison/Jay *The Federalist* (1787-1788). Essays 9, 37, 39, and 45.
J.J. Patrick, Richard C. Remy (eds.) *Lessons on the Constitution*. Washington, D.C. American Historical Association, 1985.
Nathan Glazer "Dezentralization: A Case for Self-Help." In: *Dialogue*, 1/1984.

41. Ronald Reagan "New Federalism." State of the Union Message, Jan. 20, 1982

In the same way as the German Bundeskanzler reports once a year about "die Lage der Nation", and the English Prime Minister outlines his/her annual program in the Queen's Speech, the U.S. President each January delivers the **State of the Union Message**. For this purpose Senators and Congressmen meet in a **Joint Session**.

Analyzing this speech the students will notice that Ronald Reagan (the 40th President of the U.S.A., in office since 1981) combines a report of the achievements of his presidency with an outlook on the coming year.

Terms that may need explanation:

Medicaid	a federally supported state program for persons too poor and unable to qualify for Medicare.
Medicare	a health insurance program enacted in 1965 to provide medical care for the elderly.
Aid to Families with Dependent Children (AFDC)	financial aid provided for children living with one parent or relative and lacking adequate support. This program is administered by the states with assistance of federal funds.
Food Stamps	a federal welfare program administered by state and local officials to improve nutrition in low-income families.

Discussing the **form of the speech:**
You might point out that, as Cicero explained in *De Oratore,* when speakers address an audience, their intention is either to convince or to persuade or to entertain. Sometimes all three objects may be combined in one speech.
Question: *What is Reagan's predominant intention?*
How does his style on Capitol Hill compare with his TV appearance?
In classical times, speakers used to begin their speeches with a **captatio benevolentiae.** *Does Reagan stick to his custom?* (Calling himself a 'newcomer' may serve this function. Why?)

Note also Reagan's frequent use of antithesis:

e.g. **past** policies failed:	**our** record is clear
pessimism/defeatism:	era of renewal
faith ...declining	Congress of destiny
	we cut the growth ... of Federal regulations
	we started returning power to...

repetition of words
in our excerpt, "together" occurs twice;
in the full text six times

political slogans: prosperity of the nation, peace for the world, blessings of individual liberty, grass roots (2x), faith in state and local governments, Founding Fathers etc.

In summarizing the speech, let the students explain Reagan's view of a ***new partnership****, outline what steps he took to get rid of too much bureaucracy, and to get the state and local communities more involved.*
Cf. Black Panther Program and Port Huron Statement.

■ Additional text: Federalism and the Progressive Vision.
New Partnerships, Not Abdication (Excerpt).
By Edward M. Kennedy

Edward Kennedy, U.S. Senator from Massachusetts (1980).

We understand the necessity of responding to new realities. But we also believe that rethinking our ideas must never become an excuse for retreating from our ideals.

Franklin Roosevelt was a prophet of both timeless values and changing times. Nearly half a century ago, he forged a new and creative vision of **federalism***. In the face of national problems, he summoned the entire nation to national action.

And in the past half century, Americans could not have dealt with the Depression, or met the crisis of **civil rights*** for minorities and equal rights for women, or moved toward social justice and a clean environment, if our national leaders had held to a rigid and outmoded ideology of hear-nothing, see-nothing, do-nothing federal government. Too often in the past, **states' rights*** meant neglected wrongs.

Now, more than ever, we must not retreat from this view of a vital federal role. In a society with aspirations to justice and vast geographical mobility, national standards have become a matter of decency and an imperative of public policy. The pain of hunger feels the same for a poor child in Mississippi or New York. An auto worker out of work in Detroit means lower productivity and lesser standards of life from Boston to Seattle. Polluted air and poisoned streams do not observe state and local boundaries.

So we must reject any so-called new federalism that is nothing more than a twentieth-century doctrine of **nullification*** and **secession***. It offers us only a discredited old deal that would pit state against state, city against countryside, group against group. America could no longer be one country, but instead would become a collection of narrow and contending interests, a nation literally divided against itself, with liberty and justice only for some.

At the same time, we must recognize the distinctive character of the 1980s -- and the different, more sensible possibilities of federalism. This decade can and should be a period of renaissance for state and local government; today, many Americans understand that Washington is too remote, and that decisions should be made closer to home. Progressives should not fear that feeling: for our prospects will frequently be better at the state and local level, on issues ranging from gun control to hospital cost containment.

The challenge now is to balance the imperative of national standards against the potential for state and local creativity. [...]

The Reagan New Federalism is in reality old feudalism which takes from the states and cities to make up for the federal deficit. It offers them the form of greater power, but reduces the actual power of those governments to protect their people from large and impersonal institutions. The Reagan Administration is not pro-federalism, but anti-government.

President Reagan and I agree that the federal system is not working as well as it should, and that we must strengthen it. But we disagree profoundly on the nature of the change. Where government is bad, his cure is no government; mine is better government. His program is the repeal of federal responsibility; mine is the sharing of responsibility with state and local government. To paraphrase Robert Frost, two roads diverge before us -- one leads to federal abdication, the other leads to the partnership of federalism. And the road we choose will make all the difference for our economy and our people. [...]

The full text of this speech, which Edward M. Kennedy delivered at a National Conference "Federalism: Resources and Responsibilities in the 1980's and Beyond," in Boston in May 1982 is reprinted in *American Studies Newsletter*, No. 7, Sept. 1985.

Edward M. (Ted) Kennedy is the youngest brother of the Kennedy clan. His two elder brothers, Pres. J.F. Kennedy and Robert F. Kennedy, were killed by assassins (1963 and 1968). Ted Kennedy has been U.S. Senator since 1962; he represents Massachusetts and is considered to be a liberal, progressive Democrat. His chances ever to become president of the U.S.A. vanished when a woman was killed in a car accident at Chappaquidick while Kennedy was driving. He has announced that he was not to be a candidate in the 1988 elections. However, he must still be looked upon as one of the leading figures of the Democratic Party.

Further explanations:

F.D. Roosevelt, 1882 - 1945, president of the U.S.A. for three terms (1933-45), in spite of the two-term tradition. The reason why the Americans did not stick to this convention must be seen in the crisis situation of World War II (You don't change horses in times of crisis!). Since 1951, the rule that a president can only be re-elected once has been fixed by the 22nd Amemdment. FDR took over the presidency at the time of the **Great Depression**. He fought energetically against unemployment (15m.), and in line with his **New Deal** program introduced overdue social legislation. On the way to recovery, many new federal agencies were set up with the result that - as many of his critics saw it - centralization and bureaucratization increased unduly.

nullification — a doctrine expounded by the advocates of extreme State Rights. It held that states have the right to declare null and void and to set aside in practice any law of the Federal Government which violates their voluntary compact embodied in the U.S. Constitution.

Exercises:

<u>Questions</u>

What are Edward M. Kennedy's arguments against Ronald Reagan's "New Federalism"?

Where does he agree with Reagan?

What examples from U.S. history does Kennedy present to explain the necessity of federal action?

<u>Debating</u>:

Resolved that the Federal Government (in the U.S.A. or Germany) has too much power, or

Resolved that an increase in federal power will lead to socialism, or
Resolved that as federal power increases, freedom decreases.
(Debating technique, see pp. 31ff).

B. <u>Separation of Powers and Checks and Balances</u>

In case you skipped our suggestions on 'How to get the Course started'(pp. 8ff.), you may use them at this stage to make 'government by checks and balances'clear to the students.
They should comprehend that the Founding Fathers deliberately introduced the 'checks and balances' principle in order to prevent for all time a return to the tyranny of one, a few or many. Instead of going through the Constitution paragraph by paragraph, we suggest asking them to analyse the graph and table (Students' Book pp. 116 and 117; see also additional text p. 94)

Have them list the powers of each branch of government; supply them with additional information where it seems appropriate. As a result the following data should appear on the **blackboard:**

<u>Legislature</u> (Constitution, Article 1; Amendment 17)	**Senate:** 100 Senators (two for each state, elected for six years) **House of Representatives** 435 members (in proportion to the population of each state; about 520,000 voters - one Congressman) elected for two years	elected by popular vote
Powers of Congress		see table in the Students' Book p. 117
<u>Executive</u> (Constitution, Article 2; Amendments 12,20, 22,23 and 25)	**President** elected for four years re-election possible for one second term (Amend. 20) **Vice-President** elected on presidential ticket **Cabinet** appointed by and with the consent of the Senate	
Powers of Executive		see table in the Student's Book pp. 116-117
<u>Judiciary</u> (Constitution, Article 3; Amendment 11)	**Supreme Court** 9 judges appointed for life by the President with advice and consent of the Senate	
Power of Judiciary		see table in the Students'Book pp. 116-117 see texts 5,27,30,34,35b

As some 'Bundesländer' require a separate discussion of the function of the Supreme Court, we recommend as a source for more detailed information:

Arthur S. Miller "The Supreme Court and the Living Constitution," in: *American Newsletter for Teachers of English in Germany*, Issue 34, Dec. 1968.

This is admittedly only a rough sketch of the functions and powers of the three branches of government. Not to complicate matters too much, we left out such devices as the **Electoral College**, (Amend. 12), **the Veto power of the President, the power of Congress to override a presidential veto, the possibility of impeaching a president and other officials.**
In case you want to supply your students with more information about these aspects, consult:
Helms *U.S.A. - Staat und Gesellschaft*, Hannover: Fackelträger, 8.ed.1989, Patrick/Remy *Lessons on the Constitution*, Washington D.C. American Historical Association, 1985.
Two important aspects should be mentioned:
1. The American President cannot dissolve Congress, and
2. The President cannot be removed by Congress. (cf. Great Britain and BRD)
ad point 2: use Woodrow Wilson's statement: "A Prime Minister has to govern with the majority, a President only needs to stay alive."

Conclusion:
The students should be able to explain the principle of "checks and balances", i.e. that the three branches of government share power and check each other, and have realized that their functions overlap occasionally, which from time to time has caused conflicts.
To show that the principle of the **division of powers** also applies to federal and state rights, the following table might be used:

Examples of how the Constitution divides powers:

■ Additional text:

Examples of How the Constitution Divides Powers

	TO NATIONAL GOVERNMENT	TO STATE GOVERNMENTS	TO BOTH LEVELS OF GOVERNMENT
POWERS GRANTED	To coin money To conduct foreign relations To regulate commerce with foreign nations & among states To provide an army and a navy To declare war To establish courts inferior to the Supreme Court To establish post offices To make laws necessary and proper to carry out the foregoing powers	To establish local governments To regulate commerce within a state To conduct elections To ratify amendments to the federal Constitution To take measures for public health, safety, & morals To exert powers the Constitution does not delegate to the national government or prohibit the states from using	To tax To borrow money To establish courts To make and enforce laws To charter banks and corporations To spend money for the general welfare To take private property for public purposes, with just compensation
POWERS DENIED	To tax articles exported from one state to another To violate the Bill of Rights To change state boundaries	To tax imports or exports To coin money To enter into treaties To impair obligations of contracts To abridge the privileges or immunities of citizens (14th Amendment)	To grant titles of nobility To permit slavery (13th Amendment) To deny citizens the right to vote because of race, color, or previous servitude (14th Amendment) To deny citizens the right to vote because of sex (19th Amendment)

Table adapted from Robert L. Lineberry, *Government in America* (Boston: Little, Brown and Company, 1981), p. 93.

C. Grassroots Democracy

Quite a few texts in the chapters "Separation of Church and State," "Gender and the Constitution," "Blacks and the Constitution," and "Individual Rights" (7-14, 17, 18, 20, 25, 29 and 30) revealed to what extent individual Americans, groups, and organizations have from the beginning of the American Republic made use of the principle of the Declaration of Independence that government derives its **"just power from the consent of the governed."** Not only have the Americans used their right to vote to influence the government: they have also urged it by individual or group action to listen to their demands.
Choose a couple of the above-mentioned texts to show in what cases these pressures have been effective or failed.
Let the students collect other examples, such as the Nuclear Freeze Movement, activities of Single Issue Groups etc. and have them compare these activities with German "Bürgerinitiativen".

44. The Port Huron Statement, 1962

The **Students of a Democratic Society** (SDS) date back to a convention held at Port Huron, Michigan, in June 1962. Its membership ran the gammut from center-left to communist and anarchist. It had many local chapters and an estimated activist membership of some 30,000, who were stirred up by the injustices of the northern ghettoes and the involvement of their country in the War in Vietnam, and fired by a passion to erase social and economic inequities. Some young people, esp. students, felt 'alienated.'The term alienation comprises distrust of others, esp. the government, pessimism, and occasionally self-contempt.
Donald N. Michael in *The Next Generation. The Prospects Ahead for Youth of Today and Tomorrow,* New York, Vintage Book, 1965, describes this group as

> A growing group ... of the most talented, sensitive, and searching of young adults and adolescents that will be repelled by what they interpret as politicking, commercialism, high pressure bureaucracy, and the 'big' society ...

In its heyday, SDS supported or conducted many kinds of activities such as 'sit-ins', 'teach-ins'; many of its efforts were directed towards issues related to the War in Vietnam, e.g. the draft, recruitment policies, secret research, and ties with outside agencies (see: Cox Commission Report *Crisis at Columbia*, New York, Vintage Book, 1968).
With the abolition of the draft (1973) and the end of the Vietnam War (1975), the movement petered out.
Only recently did protest return to the campus. In its issue of May 13, 1985, *Newsweek* reported "A New Breed of Activism - Protest returns to the campus - with better manners". Interestingly enough, this protest is concerned with what the SDS had fought against in the sixties: U.S. business ties with outside agencies, i.e the students requested their universities to divest their holdings in companies doing business with South Africa, thus protesting against the apartheid policy of the Republic of South Africa.

The chief concern of the **Students for a Democratic Society** was "to achieve participatory democracy."
As the first question in the Students'Book suggests, students should study closely the language used by SDS. In addition to the examples given, the following should be added:

collectively
out of isolation and into community

abolition of institutions and practices that stifle dissent
peaceful dissent actively promoted
corporations be made publicly responsible

Note also that the SDS in its statement used a lot of verbs related to action, such as

carry on, creating, bring people out,
find meaning, provide outlets, organize opposing views,
abolish, promote ...

Two further questions:
Were these demands really radical, or might they simply be called a re-interpretation of the phrase of the Declaration of Independence that "government be based on the consent of the governed"? Does the concept of "participatory democracy" of the SDS have anything in common with Ronald Reagan's idea of a "new partnership, of togetherness"?

Lit.

Kenneth Keniston *The Uncomitted.* New York: Harcourt, Brace & World, 1965.
" " *Young Radicals. Notes on Committed Youth.* New York: Harcourt, Brace & World, 1968.
Klaus Mehnert *Jugend im Zeitbruch. Woher - wohin?* Stuttgart: DVA, 1976.
On SDS and other radical groups see also:
Erwin Helms *U.S.A. - Staat und Gesellschaft.* "Radikale Gruppen der 60er Jahre", pp. 120-126 and "Die Zukunft der Parteien", pp. 132-133.

To what extent "participatory democracy" has already changed the political scene of the U.S.A. is the object of
John Naisbitt *Megatrends. Ten New Directions Transforming Our Lives.* PB New York: Warner Books, 1982/84. Esp. Chapt. 7 "Representative Democracy - Participatory Democracy", pp. 175-210.

■ Additional text: George F. Kennan "Rebels without a Program"

The distinguished diplomat and historian, George F. Kennan, in a speech before the students of Swarthmore College in 1968, attempted to bring the idealism and radicalism of the young in line with the more rational and pragmatic stance of the older generation.

> I am not saying that students should not be concerned, should not have views, should not question what goes on in the field of national policy and should not voice their questions about it. Some of us, who are older, share many of their misgivings, many of their impulses. Some of us have no less lively a sense of the dangers of the time, and are no happier than they are about a great many things that are now going on. But it lies within the power as well as the duty of all of us to recognize not only the possibility that we might be wrong but the virtual certainty that on some occasions we are bound to be. The fact that this is so does not absolve us from the duty of having views and putting them forward. But it does make it incumbent upon us to recognize the element of doubt that still surrounds the correctness of these views. And if we do that, we will not be able to lose ourselves in transports of moral indignation against those who are of opposite opinion and follow a different line; we will put our views forward only with a prayer for forgiveness for the event that we prove to be mistaken.
>
> I am aware that inhibitions and restraints of this sort on the part of us older people would be attributed by many members of the student left to a sweeping corruption of our moral integrity. Life, they would

hold, has impelled us to the making of compromises; and these compromises have destroyed the usefulness of our contribution. Crippled by our own cowardice, prisoners of the seamy adjustments we have made in order to be successfully a part of the American establishment, we are regarded as no longer capable of looking steadily into the strong clear light of truth.

In this, as in most of the reproaches with which our children shower us, there is of course an element of justification. There is a point somewhere along the way in most of our adult lives, admittedly, when enthusiasms flag, when idealism becomes tempered, when responsibility to others, and even affection for others, compels greater attention to the mundane demands of private life. There is a point when we are even impelled to place the needs of children ahead of the dictates of a defiant idealism, and to devote ourselves, pusillanimously, if you will, to the support and rearing of these same children—precisely in order that at some future date they may have the privilege of turning upon us and despising us for the materialistic faintheartedness that made their maturity possible. This, no doubt, is the nature of the compromise that millions of us make with the imperfections of government and society in our time. Many of us could wish that it might have been otherwise—that the idealistic pursuit of public causes might have remained our exclusive dedication down into later life.

But for the fact that this is not so I cannot shower myself or others with reproaches. I have seen more harm done in this world by those who tried to storm the bastions of society in the name of utopian beliefs, who were determined to achieve the elimination of all evil and the realization of the millennium within their own time, than by all the humble efforts of those who have tried to create a little order and civility and affection within their own intimate entourage, even at the cost of tolerating a great deal of evil in the public domain. Behind this modesty, after all, there has been the recognition of a vitally important truth—a truth that the Marxists, among others, have never brought themselves to recognize—namely, that the decisive seat of evil in this world is not in social and political institutions, and not even, as a rule, in the will or iniquities of statesmen, but simply in the weakness and imperfection of the human soul itself, and by that I mean literally every soul, including my own and that of the student militant at the gates. For this reason, as Tocqueville so clearly perceived when he visited this country a hundred and thirty years ago, the success of a society may be said, like charity, to begin at home. [...]

Some people, who accept our political system, believe that they have a right to disregard it and to violate the laws that have flowed from it so long as they are prepared, as a matter of conscience, to accept the penalties established for such behavior.

I am sorry; I cannot agree. The violation of law is not, in the moral and philosophic sense, a privilege that lies offered for sale with a given price tag, like an object in a supermarket, available to anyone who has the price and is willing to pay for it. It is not like the privilege of breaking crockery in a tent at the county fair for a quarter a shot. Respect for the law is not an obligation which is exhausted or obliterated by willingness to accept the penalty for breaking it.

To hold otherwise would be to place the privilege of lawbreaking preferentially in the hands of the affluent, to make respect for law a commercial proposition rather than a civic duty and to deny any authority of law independent of the sanctions established against its violation. It would then be all right for a man to create false fire alarms or frivolously to pull the emergency cord on the train, or to do any number of other things that endangered or inconvenienced other people, provided only he was prepared to accept the penalties of so doing. Surely, lawlessness and civil disobedience cannot be condoned or tolerated on this ground; and those of us who care for the good order of society have no choice but to resist attempts at its violation, when this is their only justification.

Now, being myself a father, I am only too well aware that people of my generation cannot absolve ourselves of a heavy responsibility for the state of mind in which these young people find themselves. We are obliged to recognize here, in the myopia and the crudities of *their* extremism, the reflection of our own failings: our faintheartedness and in some instances our weariness, our apathy in the face of great and obvious evils.

I am also aware that, while their methods may not be the right ones, and while their discontent may suffer in its effectiveness from the concentration on negative goals, the degree of their concern over the present state of our country and the dangers implicit in certain of its involvements is by no means exaggerated. This is a time in our national life more serious, more menacing, more crucial, than any I have ever experienced or ever hoped to experience. Not since the civil conflict of a century ago has this country, as I see it, been in such great danger; and the most excruciating aspect of this tragic state of affairs is that so much of this danger comes so largely from within, where we are giving it relatively little official attention, and so little of it comes, relatively speaking, from the swamps and jungles of Southeast Asia into which we are pouring our treasure of young blood and physical resources.

For these reasons, I do not mean to make light of the intensity of feeling by which this student left is seized. Nor do I mean to imply that people like myself can view this discontent from some sort of smug Olympian detachment, as though it were not our responsibility, as though it were not in part our own ugly and decadent face that we see in this distorted mirror. None of us could have any justification for attempting to enter into communication with these people if we did not recognize, along with the justification for their unhappiness, our own responsibility in the creation of it, and if we did not accompany our appeal to them with a profession of readiness to join them, where they want us to, in the attempt to find better answers to many of these problems.

I am well aware that in approaching them in this way and in taking issue as I have with elements of their outlook and their behavior, it is primarily myself that I have committed, not them. I know that behind all the extremisms—all the philosophical errors, all the egocentricities and all the oddities of dress and deportment—we have to do here with troubled and often pathetically appealing people, acting, however wisely or unwisely, out of sincerity and idealism, out of the unwillingness to accept a meaningless life and a purposeless society.

Well, this is not the life, and not the sort of society, that many of us would like to leave behind us in this country when our work is done. How wonderful it would be, I sometimes think to myself, if we and they—experience on the one hand, strength and enthusiasm on the other—could join forces.

Source: G.F. Kennan *Democracy and the Student Left.* New York: Atlantis-Little, Brown & Co. 1968.
Reprinted in: R.C. Bannister *american values in transition.* New York: Harcourt Brace Jovanovich, 1972. PB.

George F. Kennan served with the State Department in a variety of posts from 1926 to the sixties, e.g. as U.S. Ambassador in Moscow. His major publication is a popular study of **American Diplomacy, 1900-1950**, Chicago: University of Chicago Press, 1951. A more recent essay on U.S. diplomacy, originally published in **Foreign Affairs**, Winter 1985/86, was translated by *Die Zeit*, 21.2.1986 under the title "Die Theatralik des Moralismus vermeiden."

This is a thought-provoking speech. We have reprinted rather a long excerpt, well aware that probably only a minority of your students will be able to master it. But we deem it extremely well-suited to sum up the last two chapters. Perhaps you can use passages from it, or have a group of students deal with it and report to the class.

Questions:
1. *What is Kennan's chief criticism of the rebelling youth?*
2. *What do you think Kennan's intention was when he addressed the students of Swarthmore College?*
3. *What is his comment on the relationship between the older and the younger generation?*
4. *Would you side with Kennan or the rebelling students?* Explain.

A final quotation:
The only freedom which deserves the name, is that of pursuing our own good in our own way, so long as we do not attempt to deprive others of theirs; or impede efforts to obtain it. Each is proper guardian of his own health whether bodily or mental and spiritual. Mankind are greater gainers by suffering each other to live as seems good to themselves, than by compelling each to live as seems good to the rest.
John Stuart Mill *On Liberty*, 1859.

Conclusion (Text 45)

To get to know what American high school students think about their country's Constitution ought to be a worthwhile experience for our students. The fact that students from all over the country met for three weeks to discuss its significance is in itself quite remarkable.
Analysing the responses of American students will serve to summarize the information offered in this course.
If you want to compare the views of the young Americans with those of the older generation, use the following text:

■ Additional text: "Intent of the Framers," *Newsweek*, Oct.28,1985

Intent of the Framers

The Constitution of the United States is a design for governing, not an encyclopedia. It lays out the federal architecture, maintaining a delicate balance of forces that for nearly two centuries has kept each branch of government from running roughshod over the other two. But as a political document it is vague, even minimalist. Many questions are left unanswered. What is an unreasonable search? What is an establishment of religion? And these troubling silences provoke the greatest question of all: what does the Constitution mean? The issue is once again in the public arena, a perennial joust made unusual by new combatants: Attorney General Edwin Meese III and Supreme Court Justice William J. Brennan.

Superficially the debate is about the role history plays or should play in Supreme Court interpretations of the Constitution. How closely must courts follow the original intent of the framers? How should 18th-century words be applied to unforeseen contemporary problems? In the absence of explicit provisions, are judges free to expand the Constitution as they go along? Normally these questions would be confined to a law-school classroom, or perhaps a judge's chambers. But they've been thrust into public discourse because behind them lie some of the most practical and difficult questions the nation faces. What may police do in pursuit of criminal suspects? May public-school teachers assist students in prayer? Those issues are only part of a larger conflict over what's called judicial activism. The Reagan administration has long been unhappy that judges can and do make public policy; even before Meese took over the Justice Department it was seeking to roll back some controversial rulings. Brennan, on the other hand, is—however much he might object to the term—after 29 years the leading activist left on the Supreme Court.

The current debate began last July when, in a speech to the American Bar Association, Meese attacked several Supreme Court opinions as "bizarre" (a term borrowed from one of Chief Justice Warren Burger's dissents). He called for a return to "a jurisprudence of Original Intention. By seeking to judge policies in light of principles . . . the

Court could avoid both the charge of incoherence *and* the charge of being either too conservative or too liberal." What he meant, Meese aides said last week, was that original motive and, if necessary, historical analogy should at least limit a judge's freedom.

Tabula Rasa: On Oct. 12 Brennan counterattacked: "It is arrogant," he said in a speech at Georgetown University, "to pretend that from our vantage we can gauge accurately the intent of the framers on application of principle to specific, contemporary questions." History, he said, was only a starting point. "We current Justices read the Constitution in the only way that we can: as Twentieth Century Americans."

However history is invoked, its limitations must be recognized. The framers of the Constitution were masters of ambiguity and compromise. Insofar as they had a collective intent, it was to create a government that in effect superseded state governments. Beyond that they were careful not to be too specific. "That doesn't mean that they left a tabula rasa to be written on as a justice feels," says University of Chicago law Prof. Philip Kurland. "It means that there are several possibilities of choice for a court to make."

Consider one of the Supreme Court's "bizarre" decisions last June, in which it struck down an Alabama statute permitting moments of silence—for prayer or meditation—in public schools. By a 6-3 vote the justices declared the law unconstitutional, on the ground that it was an impermissible state establishment of religion. In dissent Justice William Rehnquist described at length the creation of the establishment clause in the First Amendment, arguing that the drafters intended only to bar the creation of a national church and not to force government into neutrality toward all religion. The Alabama law would pass muster, he concluded. The Meese forces regularly cite Rehnquist's opinion as a model of the jurisprudence of original intention.

The only problem with that approach, wrote Justice Sandra Day O'Connor in concurrence with the majority, was that the authors of the establishment clause worked in the late-18th century, before universal public education was a glimmer in Horace Mann's eye. They didn't intend *anything* about prayer in public schools. The proper course, in her view, was to apply the underlying purpose of the establishment clause: a ban on state endorsement of religion or prayer. Some moment-of-silence laws would be constitutional, she concluded, but not Alabama's, which bore a legislative history making plain the state's attempt to restore prayer to the schools.

'The People's Representatives': But if the framers are silent on a question and analogy is unhelpful, is the court entitled to act like a floating constitutional convention? According to University of Chicago law Prof. Michael McConnell, a young lawyer with the singular experience of working for both Brennan and the Reagan Justice Department: "In cases like that, the courts ought to have the humility to get out of the way and leave the decisions to the people's representatives." But apparently not always. Both Brennan and Meese have been quick to point out that the Constitution is in part an antimajoritarian document, one aimed at preserving minority rights *from* "the people's representatives." The institution with that job: the courts.

Perhaps all parties to this debate have come to rely on the courts too much. The Congress and the president are not impotent. If it is unhappy with civil-rights decisions, Congress could rewrite post-Civil War statutes that have permitted many suits to be filed. If it is impatient with affirmative action, the White House could cancel executive orders and urge Congress to reconsider the law. If it is eager to end legal abortion, Congress could pass a constitutional amendment and send it to the states. But such steps carry a political cost. It's easier to complain about the courts: they are, as has often been said, the least dangerous branch.

ARIC PRESS with ANN McDANIEL in Washington

If you want to deal with this text separately, hand out the following explanations and questions to the students.

run roughshod over	disregard, treat without understanding
minimalist	smallest or least possible (the Constitution gives the least possible specific directives)
perennial joust	recurring duel, fight
explicit	clearly set out or defined
incoherence	ideas without logical connection
supersede	replace

pass muster	be satisfactory
concurrence	agreement of opinion
glimmer	a small sign
Horace Mann	prominent American educator, lived from 1796-1859. He was of the opinion that "education is the great equalizer of man."
endorsement	to endorse=express approval
float	fluctuating as in "the floating vote" (Wechselwähler)

1. *Sum up the reporters'view of the court.*
2. *What is the difference between "judicial activism" and "judicial restraint?"*
3. *If you were a Justice of the Supreme Court which view would you favor?*
4. *Should decisions about such issues as "public prayer" be left to the people, to Congress, or to the Court?*

<u>Summary</u>

The main purpose of this summary should be to test whether the students have understood the principles underlying the **Declaration of Independence** and the **U.S. Constitution.**

They should be able to answer the following questions:

1. *What are the fundamental concepts of the Constitution?* (freedom, equality, equal protection of the law, due process of law, federalism, government by checks and balances, government based on the consent of the governed).
2. *How is the U.S. government structured?* (executive, legislature, and judiciary).
3. *How did the country become more democratic as a result of historical struggles over political power?*
4. *What were the contributions of each branch of government to keeping the Constitution flexible?*
5. *How did individuals or groups bring about changes in government policy?*
6. *Name problems that, in your opinion, a federal government is better able to solve than state governments.* (e.g. ecological problems such as pollution or the plundering of resources; sharing of funds between the rich and the poor).
7. *Does a country fare better with a written constitution or with an unwritten constitution upheld by convention?*

Finally

8. *How has it been possible to run a country on the basis of a document that was conceived two hundred years ago?*
9. *What turned the U.S. Constitution into a "living" constitution?*

The course has fulfilled its objective when the students can explain the reasons for the longevity of this document.

Such explanations should include:

1. The timeless character and validity of its principles,
2. the vagueness of its wording,
3. its flexibility, i.e. the possibility of bringing it up to date
   a. by amending it,
   b. by judicial review,
   c. by supplementing it through legislation,
4. the fact that again and again interested citizens have urged changes.

For all these reasons the U.S.A. has been able to deal successfully with situations which the Founding Fathers could not possibly have foreseen.

In another course, the class could deal with fictional literature which is concerned with the foundation of new societies, e.g.

George Orwell *Animal Farm*. Harmondsworth: Penguin PB, 1957 or

William Golding *Lord of the Flies*. London Faber & Faber, PB 1958

Selected Bibliography

Books marked with ▲ are available at the America Houses.

General

Boorstin, Daniel J. *The Genius of American Politics* Chicago University Press, 1953.

▲Boorstin, Daniel J. (ed.) *American Civilization.* New York/London: McGraw-Hill, 1972.

Bundeszentrale für Politische Bildung *Die Vereinigten Staaten von Amerika.* Informationen 211. Bonn, 1986.

▲Commager, Henry Steele (ed.) *Documents of American History.* New York: Appleton Century, Crofts, 7th ed. 1963.

▲this Constitution- *A Bicentennial Chronicle.* Washington, D.C.: Project '87.

▲Daedalus *Human Rights,* Fall 1983, Vol. 112, No.7.
Of special interest: Maurice Cranston "Are there Any Human Rights," pp. 1-18.

Friebel, Isolde & Heinrich Händel (eds.) *Britain-U.S.A, Now. A Survey in Key Words.* Frankfurt/M.: Diesterweg, 3. Aufl. 1976.

Hartig, Paul (ed.) *Amerikakunde.* In: Handbücher der Auslandskunde. Frankfurt/Main: Diesterweg, 4. Aufl. 1966.

▲Helms, Erwin *U.S.A. und Gesellschaft.* Hannover: Fackelträger, 8. Aufl. 1989.

Husemann, Richard C. & James E. Luck (eds) *Bicentennial Youth Debates. Issue Analysis.* Washington, D.C.: Speech Communication Association, 1975.

Kammen, Michael: A Machine That Would Go Itself. The Constitution in American Culture. New York: Knopf, 1986.

▲Mendelsohn, Rona "The U.S. Constitution. A Reason to Celebrate," in: *American Studies Newsletter,* No.2, Jan. 1984. Bonn: USIA.

Newsweek Education Department *Reading the Constitution.* New York: 1986
This resource unit prepared for U.S. Social Studies classes is available through Newsweek, 444 Madison Ave., New York, NY 10022. It is suitable for use in conjunction with our text collection.

▲Patrick, John L. and Richard C. Remy *Lessons on the Constitution.* Washington, D.C. American Historical Association, 1985. (A handbook for the teaching of the U.S. Constitution in U.S. High Schools. Very useful as a supplement to this course).

▲*Statistical Abstracts of the U.S.* Washington, D.C. U.S. Bureau of Census. Annual editions. (Useful for data).

▲Voice of America *Conflict in America.* Washington, D.C.: USIA-Forum Series, 1976.

▲ Welland, Dennis (ed.) *The United States. A Companion to American Studies.* London: Methuen, 1974.

Publications related to Introduction

▲ Abraham, Henry J. *Freedom and the Constitution: Civil Rights and Liberties in the U.S.* New York: Oxford University Press, 3. ed. 1977.

▲ Dworkin, Ronald *Taking Rights Seriously.* Harvard University Press, 1978.

▲ Fraenkel, Ernst *Das amerikanische Regierungssystem. Eine politische Analyse.* Köln/Opladen, 2.ed.1962.

▲ Hamilton/Madison/Jay *The Federalist or the New Constitution.* ed. by J.E. Cooke. Middleton, CO, 1961. Popular edition: Everyman's Library.

▲ Smith, Page *The Constitution, a documentary and narrative history.* New York: Morrow, 1978.

Publications related to Church and State

Cogley, John (ed.) *Religion in America. Original Essays on Religion in a Free Society.* New York: Meridian Books, 1958 (PB).

Grebenstein, S.W. (ed.) *Monkey Trial.* Boston: Houghton & Mifflin, 1960.

La Follette, M.C. (ed.) *Creationism, Science, and the Law. The Arkansas Case.* Cambridge, MA: MIT-Press, 1983.

Liebmann & Robert Wuthrow *The New Christian Right. Mobilization and Legitimation.* New York: Aldine, 1983.

Rosten, Leo (ed.) *Zu Gott führen viele Wege. Ein kurzer Führer zu Religionen in Amerika.* Bad Nauheim: Christian Verlag, 1956 (PB).

Wright, Conrad (ed.) *Religion in American Life. Selected Readings.* Boston: Houghton Mifflin, 1972 (PB).

Publications related to Gender and the Constitution

▲ *American Women: Three Decades of Change.* Washington, D.C.: Department of Commerce, Bureau of Census, 1984.

Brown, Del *Women in the Wild West.* London: New Books, 1973.

d'Aulaire, Emily and P.O. "ERA. What's it all About." *Reader's Digest*, Febr. 1977, pp. 98-102.

▲ Friedan, Betty *The Feminine Mystique.* New York: Norton, 1963.

Gould, Elsie M. *American Woman Today: Free or Frustrated?* Englewood Cliffs, N.J. Prentice-Hall, American Problems Series, 2.ed. 1977.

Judd, Barbara & Daniel Josephs *Women in the United States.* Glenville, IL.: Scott, Foresman & Co, 1975.

▲ Kendrigan, Mary Lou *Political Equality in a Democratic Society: Women in the United States*, Westport, CO.: Greenwood Press, 1984.

Kerber, Linda K & Jane de Hart Matheus *Women's America, Refocusing the Past*. Oxford University Press, 1982.

Lerner, Gerda *The Woman in American History*. Menlo Park, CA: Addison-Wesley, 1971.

Mill, John Stuart *On the Subjection of Women*, 1869. new edition-London OUP, 1966.

Scott, Anne F. (ed.) *Women in American Life*. Boston: Houghton & Mifflin, 1970.

▲ Wallace, Phyllis A. (ed.) *Women in the Workplace*. Boston: Auburn House, 1982.

▲ *Women. The Family and Freedom: The Debate and Documents, ed. by Susan G. Bell Vol. 1 (1750-1880) and 2 (1880-1950)*, Stanford University Press, 1983.

Publications related to The Constitution and the Black Population:

Blaumer, Bob (ed.) *Black Lives. White Lives*. Univ. of California Press, 1989.

Frazier, Thomas R. (ed.) *Afro-American History: Primary Sources*. New York: Harcourt, Brace & World, 1970.

▲ Fullinwinder, Robert K. *The Reverse Discrimination Controversy; a Moral and Legal Analysis*. Totowa, N.J.Rowman & Littlefield, 1980.

▲ Glazer, Nathan *Affirmative Discrimination, Ethnic Equality Public Policy*. New York: Basic Books, 1975.

Glasrud, Bruce and Alan M. Smith *Promises to Keep. A portrayal of nonwhites in the United States*. Chicago: Rand McNally & Co., 1972.

Gross Theodore *A Nation of Nations. Ethnic Literature in America*. New York: Free Press, 1971.

▲ Helms, Erwin *America Today. Black America*. Tübingen: Dt. Institut für Fernstudien, 3. Aufl. 1991.

Lapides, Frederick and David J. Burrows (eds.) *Racism. A Case Book*, New York: Crowell, 1971.

Wilson, William J. *The Truly Disadvantaged. The Inner City, the Underclass, and Public Policy*. Chicago/London, Univ. of Chicago Press, 1987.

Indians:

Spicer, Edward *A Short History of the Indians in the U.S*. New York: Van Nostrand, Co. Anvil Book, 1969.

▲ Steiner, Stan *The New Indians*. New York: Dell, A Delta Book, 1968.

Vogel, Virgil J. (ed.) *This Country Was Ours. A Documentary History of the American Indians*. New York: Harper Torchbook, 1974.

▲ Washburn, Wilcomb E. *The Indians in America*. New York: Harper Colophon Books, 1975.

Many more titles are available at the Amerika Haus Hannover and probably at others. If you are interested, ask for their list *Die Nordamerikanischen Amerikaner*.

Chinese

Sung, Betty Lee *The Story of the Chinese in America* New York: Collier Books, 3.ed. 1975.

▲Chen, Jack *The Chinese in America*. San Francisco, Harper & Row, 1980.

Japanese

▲Levine, Gene N. *The Japanese American Community: a three generation study.* New York: Praeger, 1981.

Chicanos

▲Acuna, Rodolfo *Occupied America: a history of Chicanos.* New York: Harper & Row, 1981.

Publications related to The Constitution and Other Individual Rights

"the right to bear arms"

Cline, Victor B. *Where Do You Draw the Line: An Exploration into Media Violence, Pornography and Censorship.* Salt Lake City: Brigham Young University Press, 1974

Liston, Robert *Violence in America.* New York: Messner, 1974.

Gossett, Louise Y. *Violence in Recent Southern Fiction.* Durham NC: Duke University Press, 1965.

▲*Report of the National Advisory Commission on Civil Disorders.* New York: Bantam Books, 1968.

Schlesinger, A.M. Jr. *Ideas, Power, and Violence in America.* Boston: Houghton Mifflin, 1969.

Zevin, Jack (ed.) *Violence in America. What Is the Alternative?* Englewood Cliffs, NJ, American Problems Series Prentice Hall, 2.ed. 1977.

Freedom of Speech

Chester, Lewis et.al. *Watergate. The Full Inside Story.* New York; Ballantine Books, 1973.

Commission of Freedom of the Press *A Free and Responsible Press, a general report on mass communication: newspapers, radio, motion pictures, magazines and books.* Chicago University Press, 1947.

▲Graber, Doris A. *Media Power in Politics.* Washington, D.C. Congressional Quarterly, 1984.

Gross, Gerald (ed.) *The Responsibility of the Press.* New York: Fleet Publishing Corp., 1966.

Hentoff, Nat *The First Freedom. The Tumultuous History of Free Speech in America.* New York: Delacorte Press, 1980.

▲Wise, David *The Politics of Lying: Government Deception, Secrecy, and Power.* New York: Randow House, 1973

Publications related to Basic Principles

Federalism

Bundeszentrale für politische Bildung *Föderalismus. Die Bundesrepublik Deutschland als Bundesstaat.* Bonn: BZ, Informationen 211, 1986.

Bundeszentrale für politische Bildung *Demokratie-Rechtsstaat-Sozialstaat. Strukturprinzipien der deutschen Demokratie.* Bonn: BZ, Informationen 165, 1975.

▲ Elazar, Daniel J. "Federalism in America." In: *Dialogue, No. 58. 4/1982, pp. 16-23.*

▲ Fogel, Paul D. "American Federalism." In: *American Studies Newsletter.* Bonn: USIA, 1982.

▲ Glazer, Nathan "Decentralization: A case for Self-Help." In: *Dialogue* 1/1984, pp. 2-8.

▲ Hamilton, Madison and Jay *The Federalist* New York: Mentor Books 1961 or New York: Bantam Books, 1982.

Checks and Balances

▲ Friendly, Fred and Maria J. Elliot *The Constitution: the Delicate Balance.* New York: Random, 1984.

Legislature:
Drury, Allen *Advise and Consent.* New York: Cardinal PB, 9.ed. 1968. (fiction)

Executive:
▲ America Studien/American Studies *The Reagan Administration. Eine Bilanz der ersten Amtsperiode.* ASt. Heft 4/1984.

Bernstein, Carl/Woodward, Bob *All the President's Men* Greenville, N.C.: ses, 1974.

Hersey, John *Aspects of the Presidency.* New York: Houghton Mifflin, 1980.

▲ Schlesinger, A.M. Jr. *The Imperial Presidency.* Boston: Houghton Mifflin, 1973.

▲ Warren, Robert Penn *All the King's Men.* New York: Harcourt, Brace & World, 1946. (fiction)

▲ White, Th.H. *The Making of the President, 1956-80.* New York: Cape, 1983.

Legislative:
Alsop, Stewart *The Center. People and Power in Political Washington.* New York: Popular Library, 1968.

Kirby, James C. *Congress and the Public Trust.* New York: Atheneum, 1970.

Orfield, Gay *Congressional Power: Congress and Social Change.* New York: Harcourt Brace Janovich, 1975.

Supreme Court

▲Beard, C.A. *The Supreme Court and the Constitution.* Englewood Cliffs: Prentice-Hall, 1961

▲Congressional Quarterly *Guide To The Supreme Court.* Washington, D.C.: Congressional Quarterly, 1979.

▲Lees, John D. *The President and the Supreme Court. New Deal to Watergate.* British Association for American Studies, 1980.

▲Miller, Arthur S. *The Supreme Court. Myth and Reality.* Westport, Conn.: Greenwood Press, 1976.

Grassroots Democracy

Scammon, Richard M. & Benjamin J. Wattenberg *The Real Majority- An Extraordinary Examination of the American Electorate.* New York: Coward-McCann, 1970.

<u>Media</u>

The following filmstrips and slide series are available at the **American Studies Resource Center**, Tesdorpfstr.1, 2000 Hamburg:

fc1 *America Comes of Age: A Prologue.*
Part 1: Origins "The Natural Liberty of Men"
"The Price of Liberty"
Part 2: The Frontier
"The Edge of the Wave"
"All the Good Words"

fc5 *America Comes of Age.*
Part 4: Coming of Modern Times 1890-1917
New American Women
American Challenge
Road to War

fc 63 *American Experience*
Birth of a Nation
Building of a Young Nation
One Nation Indivisible
The Rise to World Power
The Years of Boom and Bust
The Crisis of Freedom

fc 80 *U.S. Government: 200 Years of Change*
1783-1789 "We the People..."
1789-1828 "We are all Republicans"
1828-1865 "The Union Must Be Preserved"
1865-1901 "With Malice Toward None"
1901-1945 "This Nation Calls for Action"
1945-1978 "We Shall Overcome"

fc 104 *Origins of the Constitution*
The Struggle of Consensus

fc 134 *The Federal System: Checks and Balances*

fc 802 *America Comes of Age - Modern Times*

Part 1: The New American Woman
Part 2: The American Challenge
Part 3: The Road to War.

fc 820 *History of the Black in the U.S.*

Cassette Tapes 1)

▲ CT 84 *"We shall overcome"*
A documentary of the March on Washington, Aug.23, 1963 with M.L. King's complete Speech

Records

▲ *Great American Speeches*, Caedmon TC 2016
with Patrick Henry "Liberty or Death", 28.3.1775,
George Washington: First Inaugural, 30.4.1789,
Thomas Jefferson: First Inaugural, 4.3.1801,
Abraham Lincoln: The "House divided" - Speech, 17.6.1858,
Abraham Lincoln: Gettysburg Address, 19.1.1863,
W.J. Bryan: "Cross of Gold" - Speech, 8.6.1896
and others

▲ *Abraham Lincoln-Album, Caedmon TC 2015 presented by Carl Sandburg. Among the texts also A. Lincoln's First Inaugural.*

List of Resource Centers

America Houses

Amerika Haus, Hardenbergstr. 22-24, 1000 Berlin 12, Tel. 030 8197715
Amerika Haus, Staufenstr. 1, 6000 Frankfurt, Tel. 0611 722794
Amerika Haus, Tesdorpfstr. 1, 2000 Hamburg 13, Tel. 040 441061
Amerika Haus, Prinzenstr. 4, 3000 Hannover, Tel 0511 327284
Amerika Haus, Apostelnkloster 13-15, 5000 Köln 1, Tel. 0221 210366
Amerika Haus, Karolinenplatz 3, 8000 München 2, Tel. 089 595367
Amerika Haus, Friedrichstr. 23a, 7000 Stuttgart 1, Tel. 0711 210221

German-American Institutes

Carl-Schurz-Haus, Kaiser-Joseph-Str. 266, 7800 Freiburg, Tel. 0761 31645
GAI, Sophienstr. 12, 6900 Heidelberg, Tel. 06221 24771
GAI, Gleissbuehlstr. 13, 8500 Nürnberg, Tel. 0911 203327
GAI, Berliner Promenade 15, 66oo Saarbrücken, Tel. 0681 31160
GAI, Karlstr. 3, 7400 Tübingen, Tel. 07071 34071

1) only available at the Amerika Haus Hannover.

American Studies Libraries and Institutes

John F. Kennedy-Institut für Nordamerikastudien, Lansstr. 7-9, 1000 Berlin 33, Tel. 030 8381
Deutsch-Amerikanische Gesellschaft, John F. Kennedy-Haus, Kasinostr.3, 6100 Darmstadt, Tel. 06151 25924
Bibliothek der Volkshochschule, **Die Brücke**, Graf-Adolf-Str. 89, 4000 Düsseldorf 1, Tel. 0211 8993448
Britisch-Amerikanische Bibliothek, Viehoferstr. 28, 4300 Essen 1, Tel. 0201 1814145
Amerikanische Bücherei, Ständeplatz 16, 3500 Kassel, Tel. 0561 7874019
Kennedy-Haus, Holstenbrücke 2, 2300 Kiel, Tel. 0431 93279
Deutsch-Amerikanische Bibliothek, Ketzerbach 1, 3500 Marburg, Tel. 06421 67434
Deutsch-Amerikanische Institut, Haidplatz 8, 8400 Regensburg, Tel. 0941 52476
Deutsch-Amerikanische Bibliothek, Weberbach 25, 5500 Trier, Tel. 0651 7182438
Das Institut für Film und Bild in Wissenschaft und Unterricht (FWU), Bavaria-Film-Platz 3, 8022 Grünwald bei München, bietet zu allen Fernsehfilmen VCR Cassetten an. Der Verleih erfolgt durch die zuständigen Stadtbildstellen.

Bundeszentrale für politische Bildung, Berliner Freiheit 7, 5300 Bonn

American Studies Resource/Media Centers

American Studies Resource or Media Centers are essentially special collections of audiovisual media that teachers in secondary schools may find useful when teaching about the United States. The teaching materials of the centers consist primarily of filmstrips (with audio cassettes) which can be shown with the help of special projectors available on loan from the centers. In addition to the hundreds of filmstrips, the centers have varying holdings of slides, video tapes, posters, cartoons, and books. For more information, contact the American Studies Resource/ Media Center nearest to you.

American Studies Media Center
Universität Dortmund
Abteilung 15
Emil-Figge-Strasse 50
4600 **Dortmund 50**

American Studies Media Center
Pädagogische Hochschule
Sprachpraktisches Zentrum
Kunzenweg 21
7800 **Freiburg i.Br.**

American Studies Media Center
Universität Giessen
Fachbereich Anglistik
Otto-Behagel-Strasse 10B, IV
6300 **Giessen 1**

American Studies Resource Center
Amerika Haus Hamburg
Tesdorpfstrasse 1
2000 **Hamburg 13**

American Studies Media Center
Universität Regensburg
Institut für Amerikanistik
Universitätsstrasse 31
8400 **Regensburg 2**

American Studies Media Center
Universität Würzburg
Institut für Englische Philologie
Am Hubland
8700 **Würzburg**

As this book went to print, six **American Studies Resource Centers** for teachers were about to be established in the Federal Republic of Germany. Please contact an America House or German-American Institute for the address of a center in your vicinity.

Appendix

Compare the Bill of Rights with the 'Grundrechte'of the German 'Grundgesetz'.

Note the fields in which they are similar and those in which the Grundgesetz goes beyond the Bill of Rights.

What changes in modern society account for the difference?

THE DECLARATION OF INDEPENDENCE

The Second Continental Congress on June 11, 1776, appointed John Adams, Thomas Jefferson, Benjamin Franklin, Roger Sherman and Robert L. Livingston to draft a Declaration of Independence. The Declaration, primarily the work of Thomas Jefferson, was adopted by the Continental Congress in Philadelphia, on July 4, 1776. Since then that date has been the chief American political holiday—Independence Day. Upon its adoption, a copy of the Declaration, inscribed on parchment, was signed by fifty-six Members of Congress on and after August 2, 1776. The original parchment document, with signatures, is now on public view in an hermetically sealed, helium-filled glass case in the National Archives Building, Washington, D.C.

When in the Course of Human Events

it becomes necessary for one people to dissolve the political bands which have connected them with another, and to assume among the Powers of the earth, the separate and equal station to which the Laws of Nature and of Nature's God entitle them, a decent respect to the opinions of mankind requires that they should declare the causes which impel them to the separation.

We hold these truths to be self-evident, that all men are created equal, that they are endowed by their Creator with certain unalienable Rights, that among these are Life, Liberty and the pursuit of Happiness.

That to secure these rights, Governments are instituted among Men, deriving their just powers from the consent of the governed, That whenever any Form of Government becomes destructive of these ends, it is the Right of the People to alter or to abolish it, and to institute a new Government, laying its foundation on such principles, and organizing its powers in such form, as to them shall seem most likely to effect their Safety and Happiness. Prudence, indeed, will dictate that Governments long established should not be changed for light and transient causes; and accordingly all experience hath shown, that mankind are more disposed to suffer, while evils are sufferable, than to right themselves by abolishing the forms to which they are accustomed. But when a long train of abuses and usurpations, pursuing invariably the same Object evinces a design to reduce them under absolute Despotism, it is their right, it is their duty, to throw off such Government, and to provide new Guards for their future security.—Such has been the patient sufferance of these Colonies; and such is now the necessity which constrains them to alter their former Systems of Government. The history of the present King of Great Britain is a history of repeated injuries and usurpations, all having in direct object the establishment of an absolute Tyranny over these States. To prove this, let Facts be submitted to a candid world.

He has refused his Assent to Laws, the most wholesome and necessary for the public good.

He has forbidden his Governors to pass Laws of immediate and pressing importance, unless suspended in their operation till his Assent should be obtained; and when so suspended, he has utterly neglected to attend to them.

He has refused to pass other Laws for the accommodation of large districts of people, unless those people would relinquish the right of Representation in the Legislature, a right inestimable to them and formidable to tyrants only.

He has called together legislative bodies at places unusual, uncomfortable, and distant from the depository of their Public Records, for the sole purpose of fatiguing them into compliance with his measures.

He has dissolved Representative Houses repeatedly, for opposing with manly firmness his invasions on the rights of the people.

He has refused for a long time, after such dissolutions, to cause others to be elected; whereby the Legislative Powers, incapable of Annihilation, have returned to the People at large for their exercise; the State remaining in the mean time exposed to all the dangers of invasion from without, and convulsions within.

He has endeavoured to prevent the population of these States; for that purpose obstructing the Laws of Naturalization of Foreigners; refusing to pass others to encourage their migrations hither, and raising the conditions of new Appropriations of Lands.

He has obstructed the Administration of Justice, by refusing his Assent to Laws for establishing Judiciary Powers.

He has made Judges dependent on his Will alone, for

the tenure of their offices, and the amount and payment of their salaries.

He has erected a multitude of New Offices, and sent hither swarms of Officers to harrass our People, and eat out their substance.

He has kept among us, in times of peace, Standing Armies without the Consent of our legislature.

He has affected to render the Military independent of and superior to the Civil Power.

He has combined with others to subject us to a jurisdiction foreign to our constitution, and unacknowledged by our laws; giving his Assent to their acts of pretended legislation: For quartering large bodies of armed troops among us: For protecting them, by a mock Trial, from Punishment for any Murders which they should commit on the Inhabitants of these States: For cutting off our trade with all parts of the world: For imposing Taxes on us without our Consent: For depriving us in many cases, of the benefits of Trial by Jury: For transporting us beyond Seas to be tried for pretended offences: For abolishing the free System of English Laws in a neighbouring Province, establishing therein an Arbitrary government, and enlarging its Boundaries so as to render it at once an example and fit instrument for introducing the same absolute rule into these Colonies: For taking away our Charters, abolishing our most valuable Laws, and altering fundamentally the Forms of our Governments: For suspending our own Legislature, and declaring themselves invested with Power to legislate for us in all cases whatsoever.

He has abdicated Government here, by declaring us out of his Protection and waging War against us.

He has plundered our seas, ravaged our Coasts, burnt our towns, and destroyed the lives of our people.

He is at this time transporting large armies of foreign mercenaries to compleat the works of death, desolation and tyranny, already begun with circumstances of Cruelty and perfidy scarcely paralleled in the most barbarous ages, and totally unworthy the Head of a civilized nation.

He has constrained our fellow Citizens taken Captive on the high Seas to bear Arms against their Country, to become the executioners of their friends and Brethren, or to fall themselves by their Hands.

He has excited domestic insurrections amongst us, and has endeavoured to bring on the inhabitants of our frontiers, the merciless Indian Savages, whose known rule of warfare, is an undistinguished destruction of all ages, sexes and conditions.

In every stage of these Oppressions We have Petitioned for Redress in the most humble terms: Our repeated Petitions have been answered only by repeated injury. A Prince, whose character is thus marked by every act which may define a Tyrant, is unfit to be the ruler of a free People.

Nor have We been wanting in attentions to our British brethren. We have warned them from time to time of attempts by their legislature to extend an unwarrantable jurisdiction over us. We have reminded them of the circumstances of our emigration and settlement here. We have appealed to their native justice and magnanimity, and we have conjured them by the ties of our common kindred to disavow these usurpations, which, would inevitably interrupt our connections and correspondence. They too have been deaf to the voice of justice and of consanguinity. We must, therefore, acquiesce in the necessity, which denounces our Separation, and hold them, as we hold the rest of mankind, Enemies in War, in Peace Friends.

We, therefore, the Representatives of the UNITED STATES OF AMERICA, in General Congress, Assembled, appealing to the Supreme Judge of the world for the rectitude of our intentions, do, in the Name, and by Authority of the good People of these Colonies, solemnly publish and declare, That these United Colonies are, and of Right ought to be FREE AND INDEPENDENT STATES; that they are Absolved from all Allegiance to the British Crown, and that all political connection between them and the State of Great Britain, is and ought to be totally dissolved; and that as FREE AND INDEPENDENT STATES, they have full Power to levy War, conclude Peace, contract Alliances, establish Commerce, and to do all other Acts and Things which Independent States may of right do. And for the support of this Declaration, with a firm reliance on the Protection of Divine Providence, we mutually pledge to each other our Lives, our Fortunes and our sacred Honor.

John Hancock

John Adams
Samuel Adams
Josiah Bartlett
Carter Braxton
Charles Carroll of Carrollton
Samuel Chase
Abraham Clark
George Clymer
William Ellery
William Floyd
Benjamin Franklin
Elbridge Gerry
Button Gwinnett
Lyman Hall
Benjamin Harrison
John Hart
Joseph Hewes
Thomas Heyward, Jr.
William Hooper
Stephen Hopkins
Francis Hopkinson
Samuel Huntington
Thomas Jefferson
Francis Lightfoot Lee
Richard Henry Lee
Francis Lewis
Philip Livingston

Thomas Lynch, Jr.
Arthur Middleton
Thomas M'Kean
Lewis Morris
Robert Morris
John Morton
Thomas Nelson, Jr.
William Paca
Robert Treat Paine
John Penn
George Read
Caesar Rodney
George Ross
Benjamin Rush
Edward Rutledge
Roger Sherman
James Smith
Richard Stockton
Thomas Stone
George Taylor
Matthew Thornton
George Walton
William Whipple
William Williams
James Wilson
John Witherspoon
Oliver Wolcott
George Wythe

THE CONSTITUTION OF THE UNITED STATES OF AMERICA

The Constitution of the United States was drawn up by the Federal Convention of 1787 to create the system of Federal Government which began to function in America in 1789. Since then twenty-six amendments have been added. The first ten, called the Bill of Rights, were adopted in 1791. The twenty-sixth amendment was ratified on July 5, 1971. The document itself is concise and brief; its general statement of principles has made possible the extension of meanings to foster the growth of the nation from thirteen states clustered on the Atlantic side of the Allegheny Mountains in the eastern United States to a flourishing nation of fifty states spanning the North American continent and extending into the Pacific. The original document, like the Declaration of Independence, is on public view at the National Archives Building in a case designed to provide the greatest possible protection against decay.

We the People of the United States, in Order to form a more perfect Union, establish Justice, insure domestic Tranquility, provide for the common defense, promote the general Welfare, and secure the Blessings of Liberty to ourselves and our Posterity, do ordain and establish this Constitution for the United States of America.

ARTICLE ONE

Section One

All legislative powers herein granted shall be vested in a Congress of the United States, which shall consist of a Senate and House of Representatives.

Section Two

1. The House of Representatives shall be composed of members chosen every second year by the people of the several States, and the Electors in each State shall have the qualifications requisite for Electors of the most numerous branch of the State Legislature.

2. No person shall be a Representative who shall not have attained to the age of twenty-five years, and been seven years a citizen of the United States, and who shall not, when elected, be an inhabitant of that State in which he shall be chosen.

3. [Representatives and direct taxes shall be apportioned among the several States which may be included within this Union, according to their respective numbers, which shall be determined by adding to the whole number of free persons, including those bound to service for a term of years, and excluding Indians not taxed, three-fifths of all other persons.] The actual enumeration shall be made within three years after the first meeting of the Congress of the United States, and within every subsequent term of ten years, in such manner as they shall by law direct. The number of Representatives shall not exceed one for every thirty thousand, but each State shall have at least one Representative; and until such enumeration shall be made, the State of New Hampshire shall be entitled to choose three, Massachusetts eight, Rhode Island and Providence Plantations one, Connecticut five, New York six, New Jersey four, Pennsylvania eight, Delaware one, Maryland six, Virginia ten, North Carolina five, South Carolina five and Georgia, three.

4. When vacancies happen in the representation from any State, the Executive Authority thereof shall issue writs of election to fill such vacancies.

5. The House of Representatives shall choose their Speaker and other officers, and shall have the sole power of impeachment.

Section Three

1. The Senate of the United States shall be composed of two Senators from each State, chosen by the Legislature thereof, for six years; and each Senator shall have one vote.

2. Immediately after they shall be assembled in consequence of the first election, they shall be divided as equally as may be into three classes. The seats of the Senators of the first class shall be vacated at the expiration of the second year, of the second class at the expiration of the fourth year, and of the third class at the expiration of the sixth year, so that one-third may be chosen every second year; and if vacancies happen by resignation, or otherwise, during the recess of the Legislature of any State, the Executive thereof may make temporary appointments until the next meeting of the Legislature, which shall then fill such vacancies.

3. No Person shall be a Senator who shall not have attained to the age of thirty years, and been nine years a

citizen of the United States, and who shall not, when elected, be an inhabitant of that State for which he shall be chosen.

4. The Vice-President of the United States shall be President of the Senate, but shall have no vote, unless they be equally divided.

5. The Senate shall choose their other officers, and also a President *pro tempore*, in the absence of the Vice-President or when he shall exercise the Office of President of the United States.

6. The Senate shall have the sole power to try all impeachments. When sitting for that purpose, they shall be on oath or affirmation. When the President of the United States is tried, the Chief Justice shall preside: And no person shall be convicted without the concurrence of two-thirds of the members present.

7. Judgment in cases of impeachment shall not extend further than to removal from office, and disqualification to hold and enjoy any office of honor, trust, or profit under the United States: but the party convicted shall nevertheless be liable and subject to indictment, trial, judgment, and punishment, according to law.

Section Four

1. The times, places, and manner of holding elections for Senators and Representatives shall be prescribed in each State by the Legislature thereof; but the Congress may at any time by law make or alter such regulations, except as to the places of choosing Senators.

2. The Congress shall assemble at least once in every year, and such meeting shall be on the first Monday in December, unless they shall by law appoint a different day.

Section Five

1. Each House shall be the judge of the elections, returns, and qualifications of its own members, and a majority of each shall constitute a quorum to do business; but a smaller number may adjourn from day to day, and may be authorized to compel the attendance of absent members, in such manner, and under such penalties as each House may provide.

2. Each House may determine the rules of its proceedings, punish its members for disorderly behaviour, and, with the concurrence of two-thirds, expel a member.

3. Each House shall keep a journal of its proceedings, and from time to time publish the same, excepting such parts as may in their judgment require secrecy; and the yeas and nays of the members of either House on any question shall, at the desire of one-fifth of those present, be entered on the journal.

4. Neither House, during the session of Congress, shall, without the consent of the other, adjourn for more than three days, nor to any other place than that in which the two Houses shall be sitting.

Section Six

1. The Senators and Representatives shall receive a

compensation for their services, to be ascertained by law, and paid out of the Treasury of the United States. They shall in all cases, except treason, felony and breach of the peace, be privileged from arrest during their attendance at the session of their respective Houses, and in going to and returning from the same; and for any speech or debate in either House, they shall not be questioned in any other place.

2. No Senator or Representative shall, during the time for which he was elected, be appointed to any civil office under the authority of the United States, which shall have been created, or the emoluments whereof shall have been increased during such time; and no person holding any office under the United States shall be a member of either House during his continuance in office.

Section Seven

1. All bills for raising revenue shall originate in the House of Representatives, but the Senate may propose or concur with amendments, as on other bills.

2. Every bill which shall have passed the House of Representatives and the Senate shall, before it becomes a law, be presented to the President of the United States; if he approve, he shall sign it, but if not, he shall return it, with his objections, to that House in which it shall have originated, who shall enter the objections at large on their journal, and proceed to reconsider it. If after reconsideration two-thirds of that House shall agree to pass the bill, it shall be sent, together with the objections, to the other House, by which it shall likewise be reconsidered, and if approved by two-thirds of that House, it shall become a law. But in all such cases the votes of both Houses shall be determined by yeas and nays, and the names of the persons voting for and against the bill shall be entered on the journal of each House respectively. If any bill shall not be returned by the President within ten days (Sundays excepted) after it shall have been presented to him, the same shall be a law in like manner as if he had signed it, unless the Congress by their adjournment prevent its return, in which case it shall not be a law.

3. Every order, resolution or vote to which the concurrence of the Senate and House of Representatives may be necessary (except on a question of adjournment) shall be presented to the President of the United States; and before the same shall take effect, shall be approved by him, or being disapproved by him, shall be repassed by two-thirds of the Senate and the House of Representatives, according to the rules and limitations prescribed in the case of a bill.

Section Eight

1. The Congress shall have power: To lay and collect taxes, duties, imposts, and excises, to pay the debts and provide for the common defense and general welfare of the United States; but all duties, imposts, and excises shall be uniform throughout the United States;

2. To borrow money on the credit of the United States;

3. To regulate commerce with foreign nations, and among the several States, and with the Indian tribes;

4. To establish a uniform rule of naturalization, and uniform laws on the subject of bankruptcies throughout the United States;

5. To coin money, regulate the value thereof, and of foreign coin, and fix the standard of weights and measures;

6. To provide for the punishment of counterfeiting the securities and current coin of the United States;

7. To establish Post Offices and Post Roads;

8. To promote the progress of science and useful arts, by securing for limited times to authors and inventors the exclusive right to their respective writings and discoveries;

9. To constitute tribunals inferior to the Supreme Court;

10. To define and punish piracies and felonies committed on the high seas, and offenses against the law of nations;

11. To declare war, grant letters of marque and reprisal, and make rules concerning captures on land and water;

12. To raise and support armies, but no appropriation of money to that use shall be for a longer term than two years;

13. To provide and maintain a navy;

14. To make rules for the government and regulation of the land and naval forces;

15. To provide for calling forth the militia to execute the laws of the Union, suppress insurrections and repel invasions;

16. To provide for organizing, arming, and disciplining the militia, and for governing such part of them as may be employed in the service of the United States, reserving to the States respectively, the appointment of the officers, and the authority of training the militia according to the discipline prescribed by Congress;

17. To exercise exclusive legislation in all cases whatsoever, over such District (not exceeding ten miles square) as may, by cession of particular States, and the acceptance of Congress, become the seat of Government of the United States, and to exercise like authority over all places purchased by the consent of the Legislature of the State in which the same shall be, for the erection of forts, magazines, arsenals, dock-yards, and other needful buildings;—And

18. To make all laws which shall be necessary and proper for carrying into execution the foregoing powers, and all other powers vested by this Constitution in the Government of the United States, or in any department or officer thereof.

Section Nine

1. The migration or importation of such persons as any

of the States now existing shall think proper to admit, shall not be prohibited by the Congress prior to the year one thousand eight hundred and eight, but a tax or duty may be imposed on such importation, not exceeding ten dollars for each person.

2. The privilege of the Writ of Habeas Corpus shall not be suspended, unless when in the cases of rebellion or invasion the public safety may require it.

3. No Bill of Attainder or *ex post facto* law shall be passed.

4. No capitation, or other direct tax shall be laid, unless in proportion to the census or enumeration herein before directed to be taken.

5. No tax or duty shall be laid on articles exported from any State.

6. No preference shall be given by any regulation of commerce or revenue to the ports of one State over those of another, nor shall vessels bound to, or from, one State, be obliged to enter, clear, or pay duties in another.

7. No money shall be drawn from the Treasury but in consequence of appropriations made by law; and a regular statement and account of the receipts and expenditures of all public money shall be published from time to time.

8. No title of nobility shall be granted by the United States: And no person holding any office of profit or trust under them, shall, without the consent of the Congress, accept of any present, emolument, office, or title of any kind whatever, from any king, prince, or foreign State.

Section Ten

1. No State shall enter into any treaty, alliance, or confederation, grant letters of marque and reprisal, coin money, emit bills of credit, make anything but gold and silver coin a tender in payment of debts, pass any Bill of Attainder, *ex post facto* law, or law impairing the obligation of contracts, or grant any title of nobility.

2. No State shall, without the consent of the Congress, lay any impost or duties on imports or exports, except what may be absolutely necessary for executing its inspection laws, and the net produce of all duties and imposts, laid by any State on imports or exports, shall be for the use of the Treasury of the United States; and all such laws shall be subject to the revision and control of the Congress.

3. No State shall, without the consent of Congress, lay any duty of tonnage, keep troops, or ships of war in time of peace, enter into any agreement or compact with another State, or with a foreign power, or engage in war, unless actually invaded, or in such imminent danger as will not admit of delay.

ARTICLE TWO

Section One

1. The Executive power shall be vested in a President of

the United States of America. He shall hold his office during the term of four years, and, together with the Vice-President, chosen for the same term, be elected, as follows:

2. Each State shall appoint, in such manner as the Legislature thereof may direct, a number of Electors, equal to the whole number of Senators and Representatives to which the State may be entitled in the Congress; but no Senator or Representative, or person holding an office of trust or profit under the United States, shall be appointed an Elector.

(The Electors shall meet in their respective States, and vote by ballot for two persons, of whom one at least shall not be an inhabitant of the same State with themselves. And they shall make a list of all the persons voted for, and of the number of votes for each; which list they shall sign and certify, and transmit sealed to the seat of the Government of the United States, directed to the President of the Senate. The President of the Senate shall, in the presence of the Senate and House of Representatives, open all the certificates, and the votes shall then be counted. The person having the greatest number of votes shall be the President, if such number be a majority of the whole number of Electors appointed; and if there be more than one who have such majority, and have an equal number of votes, then the House of Representatives shall immediately choose by ballot one of them for President; and if no person have a majority, then from the five highest on the list the said House shall in like manner choose the President. But in choosing the President, the votes shall be taken by States, the representation from each State having one vote; a quorum, for this purpose, shall consist of a member or members from two-thirds of the States, and a majority of all the States shall be necessary to a choice. In every case, after the choice of the President, the person having the greatest number of votes of the Electors shall be the Vice-President. But if there should remain two or more who have equal votes, the Senate shall choose from them by ballot the Vice-President.)*

3. The Congress may determine the time of choosing the Electors, and the day on which they shall give their votes; which day shall be the same throughout the United States.

4. No person except a natural born citizen, or a citizen of the United States at the time of the adoption of this Constitution, shall be eligible to the office of the President; neither shall any person be eligible to that office who shall not have attained to the age of thirty-five years, and been fourteen years a resident within the United States.

5. In case of the removal of the President from office, or of his death, resignation, or inability to discharge the powers and duties of the said office, the same shall devolve on the Vice-President, and the Congress may by law provide for the case of removal, death, resignation, or inability, both of the President and Vice-President, declaring what officer shall then act as President,

---

* This article has been superseded by Amendment XII, page 33

and such officer shall act accordingly until the disability be removed or a President shall be elected.

6. The President shall, at stated times, receive for his services a compensation which shall neither be increased nor diminished during the period for which he shall have been elected, and he shall not receive within that period any other emolument from the United States, or any of them.

7. Before he enter on the execution of his office, he shall take the following oath or affirmation:—'I do solemnly swear (or affirm) that I will faithfully execute the Office of President of the United States, and will, to the best of my ability, preserve, protect, and defend the Constitution of the United States.'

Section Two

1. The President shall be Commander-in-Chief of the Army and Navy of the United States, and of the militia of the several States, when called into the actual service of the United States; he may require the opinion, in writing, of the principal officer in each of the Executive Departments upon any subject relating to the duties of their respective offices, and he shall have power to grant reprieves and pardons for offenses against the United States, except in cases of impeachment.

2. He shall have power, by and with the advice and consent of the Senate, to make treaties, provided two-thirds of the Senators present concur; and he shall nominate, and by and with the advice and consent of the Senate, shall appoint Ambassadors, other public Ministers and Consuls, Judges of the Supreme Court, and all other officers of the United States, whose appointments are not herein otherwise provided for, and which shall be established by law; but the Congress may by law vest the appointment of such inferior officers, as they think proper, in the President alone, in the courts of law, or in the heads of departments.

3. The President shall have power to fill up all vacancies that may happen during the recess of the Senate by granting commissions, which shall expire at the end of their next session.

Section Three

He shall from time to time give to the Congress information of the State of the Union, and recommend to their consideration such measures as he shall judge necessary and expedient; he may, on extraordinary occasions, convene both Houses, or either of them, and in case of disagreement between them with respect to the time of adjournment, he may adjourn them to such time as he shall think proper; he shall receive Ambassadors and other public Ministers; he shall take care that the laws be faithfully executed, and shall commission all the officers of the United States.

Section Four

The President, Vice-President, and all civil officers of the United States, shall be removed from office on impeachment for, and conviction of, treason, bribery, or other high crimes and misdemeanors.

ARTICLE THREE

Section One

The judicial power of the United States shall be vested in one Supreme Court, and in such inferior courts as the Congress may from time to time ordain and establish. The Judges, both of the Supreme and inferior courts, shall hold their offices during good behaviour, and shall, at stated times, receive for their services a compensation, which shall not be diminished during their continuance in office.

Section Two

1. The judicial power shall extend to all cases, in law and equity, arising under this Constitution, the laws of the United States, and treaties made, or which shall be made, under their authority; to all cases affecting Ambassadors, other public Ministers and Consuls; to all cases of admiralty and maritime jurisdiction; to controversies to which the United States shall be a party; to controversies between two or more States, between a State and citizens of another State, between citizens of different States; between citizens of the same State claiming lands under grants of different States, and between a State, or the citizens thereof, and foreign States, citizens, or subjects.

2. In all cases affecting Ambassadors, other public Ministers and Consuls, and those in which a State shall be party, the Supreme Court shall have original jurisdiction. In all the other cases before mentioned, the Supreme Court shall have appellate jurisdiction, both as to law and fact, with such exceptions, and under such regulations as the Congress shall make.

3. The trial of all crimes, except in cases of impeachment, shall be by jury, and such trial shall be held in the State where the said crimes shall have been committed; but when not committed within any State, the trial shall be at such place or places as the Congress may by law have directed.

Section Three

1. Treason against the United States shall consist only in levying war against them, or in adhering to their enemies, giving them aid and comfort. No person shall be convicted of treason unless on the testimony of two witnesses to the same overt act, or on confession in open court.

2. The Congress shall have power to declare the punishment of treason, but no attainder of treason shall work corruption of blood or forfeiture except during the life of the person attainted.

ARTICLE FOUR

Section One

Full faith and credit shall be given in each State to the

public acts, records, and judicial proceedings of every other State. And the Congress may by general laws prescribe the manner in which such acts, records, and proceedings shall be proved, and the effect thereof.

Section Two

1. The citizens of each State shall be entitled to all privileges and immunities of citizens in the several States.

2. A person charged in any State with treason, felony or other crime, who shall flee from justice, and be found in another State, shall on demand of the executive authority of the State from which he fled, be delivered up, to be removed to the State having jurisdiction of the crime.

3. No person held to service or labour in one State under the laws thereof, escaping into another, shall in consequence of any law or regulation therein, be discharged from such service or labour, but shall be delivered up on claim of the party to whom such service or labour may be due.

Section Three

1. New States may be admitted by the Congress into this Union; but no new State shall be formed or erected within the jurisdiction of any other State; nor any State be formed by the junction of two or more States, or parts of States, without the consent of the Legislatures of the States concerned as well as of the Congress.

2. The Congress shall have power to dispose of and make all needful rules and regulations respecting the territory or other property belonging to the United States; and nothing in this Constitution shall be so construed as to prejudice any claims of the United States, or of any particular State.

Section Four

The United States shall guarantee to every State in this Union a Republican form of government, and shall protect each of them against invasion; and on application of the Legislature, or of the Executive (when the Legislature cannot be convened) against domestic violence.

ARTICLE FIVE

The Congress, whenever two-thirds of both Houses shall deem it necessary, shall propose amendments to this Constitution, or, on the application of the legislatures of two-thirds of the several States, shall call a convention for proposing amendments, which, in either case, shall be valid to all intents and purposes, as part of this Constitution, when ratified by the Legislatures of three-fourths of the several States, or by conventions in three-fourths thereof, as the one or the other mode of ratification may be proposed by the Congress; provided that no amendment which may be made prior to the year one thousand eight hundred and eight shall in any manner affect the first and fourth clauses in the Ninth Section of the First Article; and that no State, without its consent shall be deprived of its equal suffrage in the Senate.

ARTICLE SIX

1. All debts contracted and engagements entered into before the adoption of this Constitution, shall be as valid against the United States under this Constitution as under the Confederation.

2. This Constitution, and the laws of the United States which shall be made in pursuance thereof; and all treaties made, or which shall be made, under the authority of the United States, shall be the supreme law of the land; and the Judges in every State shall be bound thereby, anything in the Constitution or laws of any State to the contrary notwithstanding.

3. The Senators and Representatives before mentioned, and the members of the several State Legislatures, and all Executive and Judicial Officers, both of the United States and of the several States, shall be bound by oath or affirmation, to support this Constitution; but no religious test shall ever be required as a qualification to any office or public trust under the United States.

ARTICLE SEVEN

The ratification of the Conventions of nine States, shall be sufficient for the establishment of this Constitution between the States so ratifying the same.

Done in Convention by the Unanimous Consent of the States present the Seventeenth Day of September in the Year of our Lord one thousand seven hundred and eighty-seven, and of the Independence of the United States of America the twelfth. In Witness whereof We have hereunto subscribed our names.

G Washington
President and deputy from Virginia.

NEW HAMPSHIRE
John Langdon
Nicholas Gilman

MASSACHUSETTS
Nathaniel Gorham
Rufus King

CONNECTICUT
Wm. Saml. Johnson
Roger Sherman

NEW YORK
Alexander Hamilton

NEW JERSEY
Wil. Livingston
David Brearley
Wm. Paterson
Jona Dayton

DELAWARE
Geo. Read
Gunning Bedford jun
John Dickinson
Richard Bassett
Jaco. Broom

MARYLAND
James McHenry
Dan of St Thos Jenifer
Danl Carroll

VIRGINIA
John Blair
James Madison Jr.

NORTH CAROLINA
Wm. Blount
Richd. Dobbs Spaight
Hu Williamson

PENNSYLVANIA
B Franklin
Thomas Mifflin
Robt Morris
Geo. Clymer
Thos. Fitzsimons
Jared Ingersoll
James Wilson
Gouv Morris

SOUTH CAROLINA
J. Rutledge
Charles Cotesworth Pinckney
Charles Pinckney
Pierce Butler

GEORGIA
William Few
Abr Baldwin

Attest. **William Jackson, Secretary**

Articles in Addition to, and Amendment of, *the Constitution of the United States of America, proposed by Congress, and ratified by the Legislatures of the Several States pursuant to the Fifth Article of the Original Constitution:*

ARTICLE ONE

Congress shall make no law respecting an establishment of religion, or prohibiting the free exercise thereof; or abridging the freedom of speech, or of the press; or the right of the people peaceably to assemble, and to petition the Government for a redress of grievances.

ARTICLE TWO

A well-regulated militia, being necessary to the security of a free State, the right of the people to keep and bear arms, shall not be infringed.

ARTICLE THREE

No soldier shall, in time of peace, be quartered in any house, without the consent of the owner, nor in time of war, but in a manner to be prescribed by law.

ARTICLE FOUR

The right of the people to be secure in their persons, houses, papers, and effects, against unreasonable searches and seizures, shall not be violated, and no warrants shall issue, but upon probable cause, supported by oath or affirmation, and particularly describing the place to be searched, and the persons or things to be seized.

ARTICLE FIVE

No person shall be held to answer for a capital, or other infamous crime, unless on a presentment or indictment of a Grand Jury, except in cases arising in the land or naval forces, or in the militia, when in actual service, in time of war or public danger; nor shall any person be subject for the same offense to be twice put in jeopardy of life or limb; nor shall be compelled in any criminal case to be a witness against himself; nor be deprived of life, liberty, or property, without due process of law; nor shall private property be taken for public use, without just compensation.

ARTICLE SIX

In all criminal prosecutions, the accused shall enjoy the right to a speedy and public trial, by an impartial jury of the State and district wherein the crime shall have been committed, which district shall have been previously ascertained by law, and to be informed of the nature and cause of the accusation; to be confronted with witness against him; to have compulsory process for obtaining witnesses in his favour, and to have the assistance of counsel for his defense.

ARTICLE SEVEN

In suits at common law, where the value in controversy shall exceed twenty dollars, the right of trial by jury shall be preserved, and no fact tried by a jury shall be otherwise re-examined in any court of the United States, than according to the rules of the common law.

ARTICLE EIGHT

Excessive bail shall not be required, nor excessive fines imposed, nor cruel and unusual punishments inflicted.

ARTICLE NINE

The enumeration in the Constitution, of certain rights shall not be construed to deny or disparage others retained by the people.

ARTICLE TEN

The powers not delegated to the United States by the Constitution, nor prohibited by it to the States, are reserved to the States respectively, or to the people.

ARTICLE ELEVEN

The judicial power of the United States shall not be construed to extend to any suit in law or equity, commenced or prosecuted against one of the United States by citizens of another State, or by citizens or subjects of any foreign State.

ARTICLE TWELVE

The electors shall meet in their respective States, and vote by ballot for President and Vice-President, one of whom at least shall not be an inhabitant of the same State with themselves; they shall name in their ballots the person voted for as President, and in distinct ballots the person voted for as Vice-President, and they shall make distinct lists of all persons voted for as President, and of all persons voted for as Vice-President, and of the number of votes for each, which lists they shall sign and certify, and transmit sealed to the seat of the Government of the United States, directed to the President of the Senate; the President of the Senate shall, in the presence of the Senate and House of Representatives, open all the certificates and the votes shall then be counted; the person having the greatest number of votes for President, shall be the President, if such number be a majority of the whole number of electors appointed; and if no person have such majority, then from the persons having the highest numbers not exceeding three on the list of those voted for as President, the House of Representatives shall choose immediately, by ballot, the President. But in choosing the President, the votes shall be taken by States, the representation from each State having one vote; a quorum for this purpose shall consist of a member or members from two-thirds of the States, and a majority of all the States shall be necessary to a choice. And if the House of Representatives shall not choose a President whenever the right of choice shall devolve upon them, before the fourth day of March next following, then the Vice-President shall act as President, as in the case of the death or other constitutional disability of the President. The person having the greatest number of votes as Vice-President, shall be the Vice-President, if such number be a majority of the whole number of Electors appointed, and if no person have a majority, then from the two highest numbers on the list, the Senate shall choose the Vice-President; a quorum for the purpose shall consist of two-thirds of the whole number of Senators, and a majority of the whole number shall be necessary to a choice. But no person constitutionally ineligible to the office of President shall be eligible to that of Vice-President of the United States.

ARTICLE THIRTEEN

1. Neither slavery nor involuntary servitude, except as a punishment for crime whereof the party shall have been duly convicted, shall exist within the United States, or any place subject to their jurisdiction.

2. Congress shall have power to enforce this article by appropriate legislation.

ARTICLE FOURTEEN

1. All persons born or naturalized in the United States, and subject to the jurisdiction thereof, are citizens of the United States and of the State wherein they reside. No State shall make or enforce any law which shall abridge the privileges or immunities of citizens of the United States; nor shall any State deprive any person of life, liberty, or property, without due process of law; nor deny to any person within its jurisdiction the equal protection of the laws.

2. Representatives shall be apportioned among the several States according to their respective numbers, counting the whole number of persons in each State, excluding Indians not taxed. But when the right to vote at any election for the choice of Electors for President and Vice-President of the United States, representatives in Congress, the Executive and Judicial officers of a State, or the members of the Legislature thereof, is denied to any of the male members of such State, being twenty-one years of age, and citizens of the United States, or in any way abridged, except for participation in rebellion, or other crimes, the basis of representation therein shall be reduced in the proportion which the number of such male citizens shall bear to the whole number of male citizens twenty-one years of age in such State.

3. No person shall be a Senator or Representative in Congress, or Elector of President and Vice-President, or hold any office, civil or military, under the United States, or under any State, who, having previously taken an oath, as a member of Congress, or as an officer of the United States, or as a member of any State Legislature, or as an Executive or Judicial officer of any State, to support the Constitution of the United States, shall have engaged in insurrection or rebellion against the same, or given aid and comfort to the enemies thereof. But Congress may, by a vote of two-thirds of each House, remove such disability.

4. The validity of the public debt of the United States, authorized by law, including debts incurred for payment of pensions and bounties for services in suppressing insurrection and rebellion, shall not be questioned. But neither the United States nor any State shall assume or pay any debt or obligation incurred in aid of insurrection or rebellion against the United States, or any claim for the loss or emancipation of any slave; but all such debts, obligations, and claims shall be held illegal and void.

5. Congress shall have power to enforce by appropriate legislation the provisions of this article.

ARTICLE FIFTEEN

1. The right of citizens of the United States to vote shall not be denied or abridged by the United States or by any State on account of race, color, or previous condition of servitude.

2. The Congress shall have power to enforce this article by appropriate legislation.

ARTICLE SIXTEEN

The Congress shall have power to lay and collect taxes on incomes, from whatever sources derived, without apportionment among the several States, and without regard to any census or enumeration.

ARTICLE SEVENTEEN

1. The Senate of the United States shall be composed of two Senators from each State, elected by the people thereof, for six years; and each Senator shall have one vote. The Electors in each State shall have the qualifications requisite for Electors of the most numerous branch of the State Legislatures.

2. When vacancies happen in the representation of any State in the Senate, the Executive authority of such State shall issue writs of election to fill such vacancies: Provided, That the legislature of any State may empower the Executive thereof to make temporary appointments until the people fill the vacancies by election as the legislature may direct.

3. This amendment shall not be so construed as to affect the election or term of any Senator chosen before it becomes valid as part of the Constitution.

ARTICLE EIGHTEEN

1. After one year from the ratification of this article

the manufacture, sale or transportation of intoxicating liquors within, the importation thereof into, or the exportation thereof from the United States and all territory subject to the jurisdiction thereof for beverage purposes is hereby prohibited.

2. The Congress and the several States shall have concurrent power to enforce this article by appropriate legislation.

3. This article shall be inoperative unless it shall have been ratified as an amendment to the Constitution by the Legislatures of the several States, as provided in the Constitution, within seven years from the date of the submission hereof to the States by the Congress.

ARTICLE NINETEEN

1. The right of citizens of the United States to vote shall not be denied or abridged by the United States or by any State on account of sex.

2. Congress shall have power to enforce this article by appropriate legislation.

ARTICLE TWENTY

1. The terms of the President and Vice-President shall end at noon on the 20th day of January, and the terms of Senators and Representatives at noon on the 3rd day of January, of the years in which such terms would have ended if this article had not been ratified; and the terms of their successors shall then begin.

2. The Congress shall assemble at least once in every year, and such meeting shall begin at noon on the 3rd day of January, unless they shall by law appoint a different day.

3. If, at the time fixed for the beginning of the term of the President, the President elect shall have died, the Vice-President elect shall become President. If a President shall not have been chosen before the time fixed for the beginning of his term, or if the President elect shall have failed to qualify, then the Vice-President elect shall act as President until a President shall have qualified; and the Congress may by law provide for the case wherein neither a President elect nor a Vice-President elect shall have qualified, declaring who shall then act as President, or the manner in which one who is to act shall be selected, and such person shall act accordingly until a President or Vice-President shall have qualified.

4. The Congress may by law provide for the case of death of any of the persons from whom the House of Representatives may choose a President whenever the right of choice shall have devolved upon them, and for the case of the death of any of the persons from whom the Senate may choose a Vice-President whenever the right of choice shall have devolved upon them.

5. Sections 1 and 2 shall take effect on the 15th day of October following the ratification of this article.

6. This article shall be inoperative unless it shall have been ratified as an amendment to the Constitution by

the Legislatures of three-fourths of the several States within seven years from the date of its submission.

ARTICLE TWENTY-ONE

1. The eighteenth article of amendment to the Constitution of the United States is hereby repealed.

2. The transportation or importation into any State, Territory, or possession of the United States for delivery or use therein of intoxicating liquors in violation of the laws thereof, is hereby prohibited.

3. This article shall be inoperative unless it shall have been ratified as an amendment to the Constitution by conventions in the several States, as provided in the Constitution, within seven years from the date of the submission hereof to the States by the Congress.

ARTICLE TWENTY-TWO

1. No person shall be elected to the office of the President more than twice, and no person who has held the office of President, or acted as President, for more than two years of a term to which some other person was elected President shall be elected to the office of the President more than once. But this Article shall not apply to any person holding the office of President when this Article was proposed by the Congress, and shall not prevent any person who may be holding the office of President, or acting as President, during the term within which this Article becomes operative, from holding the office of President or acting as President during the remainder of such term.

2. This article shall be inoperative unless it shall have been ratified as an amendment to the Constitution by the Legislatures of three-fourths of the several States within seven years from the date of its submission to the States by the Congress.

ARTICLE TWENTY-THREE

1. The District constituting the seat of Government of the United States shall appoint in such manner as the Congress may direct:

A number of electors of President and Vice-President equal to the whole number of Senators and Representatives in Congress to which the District would be entitled if it were a State, but in no event more than the least populous State; they shall be in addition to those appointed by the States, but they shall be considered, for the purposes of the election of the President and Vice-President, to be electors appointed by a State; and they shall meet in the District and perform such duties as provided by the twelfth article of amendment.

2. The Congress shall have power to enforce this article by appropriate legislation.

ARTICLE TWENTY-FOUR

1. The right of citizens of the United States to vote in any primary or other election for President or Vice-

President, for electors for President or Vice-President, or for Senator or Representative in Congress, shall not be denied or abridged by the United States or any State by reason of failure to pay any poll tax or other tax.

2. The Congress shall have power to enforce this article by appropriate legislation.

ARTICLE TWENTY-FIVE

Section 1. In case of the removal of the President from office or his death or resignation, the Vice-President shall become President.

Section 2. Whenever there is a vacancy in the office of the Vice-President, the President shall nominate a Vice-President who shall take the office upon confirmation by a majority vote of both houses of Congress.

Section 3. Whenever the President transmits to the President pro tempore of the Senate and the Speaker of the House of Representatives his written declaration that he is unable to discharge the powers and duties of his office, and until he transmits to them a written declaration to the contrary, such powers and duties shall be discharged by the Vice-President as Acting President.

Section 4. Whenever the Vice-President and a majority of either the principal officers of the executive departments, or of such other body as Congress may by law provide, transmit to the President pro tempore of the Senate and the Speaker of the House of Representatives their written declaration that the President is unable to discharge the powers and duties of his office, the Vice President shall immediately assume the powers and duties of the office as Acting President.

Thereafter, when the President transmits to the President pro tempore of the Senate and the Speaker of the House of Representatives his written declaration that no inability exists, he shall resume the powers and duties of his office unless the Vice President and a majority of either the principal officers of the executive department, or of such other body as Congress may by law provide, transmit within four days to the President pro tempore of the Senate and the Speaker of the House of Representatives their written declaration that the President is unable to discharge the powers and duties of his office. Thereupon Congress shall decide the issue, assembling within 48 hours for that purpose if not in session. If the Congress, within 21 days after receipt of the latter written declaration, or, if Congress is not in session, within 21 days after Congress is required to assemble, determines by two-thirds vote of both houses that the President is unable to discharge the powers and duties of his office, the Vice President shall continue to discharge the same as Acting President; otherwise, the President shall resume the powers and duties of his office.

ARTICLE TWENTY-SIX

Section 1. The right of citizens of the United States, who are eighteen years of age or older, to vote shall not be denied or abridged by the United States or by any State on account of age.

Section 2. The Congress shall have power to enforce this article by appropriate legislation.

Grundgesetz für die Bundesrepublik Deutschland

vom 23. Mai 1949 [1])

Präambel

Im Bewußtsein seiner Verantwortung vor Gott und den Menschen, von dem Willen beseelt, seine nationale und staatliche Einheit zu wahren und als gleichberechtigtes Glied in einem vereinten Europa dem Frieden der Welt zu dienen, hat das deutsche Volk

in den Ländern Baden, Bayern, Bremen, Hamburg, Hessen, Niedersachsen, Nordrhein-Westfalen, Rheinland-Pfalz, Schleswig-Holstein, Württemberg-Baden und Württemberg-Hohenzollern,

um dem staatlichen Leben für eine Übergangszeit eine neue Ordnung zu geben,

kraft seiner verfassungsgebenden Gewalt dieses Grundgesetz der Bundesrepublik Deutschland beschlossen.

Es hat auch für jene Deutschen gehandelt, denen mitzuwirken versagt war.

Das gesamte deutsche Volk bleibt aufgefordert, in freier Selbstbestimmung die Einheit und Freiheit Deutschlands zu vollenden.

I. Die Grundrechte

Artikel 1

(1) Die Würde des Menschen ist unantastbar. Sie zu achten und zu schützen ist Verpflichtung aller staatlichen Gewalt.

(2) Das deutsche Volk bekennt sich darum zu unverletzlichen und unveräußerlichen Menschenrechten als Grundlage jeder menschlichen Gemeinschaft, des Friedens und der Gerechtigkeit in der Welt.

(3) Die nachfolgenden Grundrechte binden Gesetzgebung, vollziehende Gewalt und Rechtsprechung als unmittelbar geltendes Recht [1]).

Artikel 2

(1) Jeder hat das Recht auf die freie Entfaltung seiner Persönlichkeit, soweit er nicht die Rechte anderer verletzt und nicht gegen die verfassungsmäßige Ordnung oder das Sittengesetz verstößt.

(2) Jeder hat das Recht auf Leben und körperliche Unversehrtheit. Die Freiheit der Person ist unverletzlich. In diese Rechte darf nur auf Grund eines Gesetzes eingegriffen werden.

Artikel 3

(1) Alle Menschen sind vor dem Gesetz gleich.

(2) Männer und Frauen sind gleichberechtigt.

(3) Niemand darf wegen seines Geschlechtes, seiner Abstammung, seiner Rasse, seiner Sprache, seiner Heimat und Herkunft, seines Glaubens, seiner religiösen oder politischen Anschauungen benachteiligt oder bevorzugt werden.

Artikel 4

(1) Die Freiheit des Glaubens, des Gewissens und die Freiheit des religiösen und weltanschaulichen Bekenntnisses sind unverletzlich.

(2) Die ungestörte Religionsausübung wird gewährleistet.

(3) Niemand darf gegen sein Gewissen zum Kriegsdienst mit der Waffe gezwungen werden. Das Nähere regelt ein Bundesgesetz.

Artikel 5

(1) Jeder hat das Recht, seine Meinung in Wort, Schrift und Bild frei zu äußern und zu verbreiten und sich aus allgemein zugänglichen Quellen ungehindert zu unterrichten. Die Pressefreiheit und die Freiheit der Berichterstattung durch Rundfunk und Film werden gewährleistet. Eine Zensur findet nicht statt.

(2) Diese Rechte finden ihre Schranken in den Vorschriften der allgemeinen Gesetze, den gesetzlichen Bestimmungen zum Schutze der Jugend und in dem Recht der persönlichen Ehre.

(3) Kunst und Wissenschaft, Forschung und Lehre sind frei. Die Freiheit der Lehre entbindet nicht von der Treue zur Verfassung.

Artikel 6

(1) Ehe und Familie stehen unter dem besonderen Schutz der staatlichen Ordnung.

(2) Pflege und Erziehung der Kinder sind das natürliche Recht der Eltern und die zuvörderst ihnen obliegende Pflicht. Über ihre Betätigung wacht die staatliche Gemeinschaft.

(3) Gegen den Willen der Erziehungsberechtigten dürfen Kinder nur auf Grund eines Gesetzes von der Familie getrennt werden, wenn die Erziehungsberechtigten versagen oder wenn die Kinder aus anderen Gründen zu verwahrlosen drohen.

(4) Jede Mutter hat Anspruch auf den Schutz und die Fürsorge der Gemeinschaft.

(5) Den unehelichen Kindern sind durch die Gesetzgebung die gleichen Bedingungen für ihre leibliche und seelische Entwicklung und ihre Stellung in der Gesellschaft zu schaffen wie den ehelichen Kindern.

Artikel 7

(1) Das gesamte Schulwesen steht unter der Aufsicht des Staates.

(2) Die Erziehungsberechtigten haben das Recht, über die Teilnahme des Kindes am Religionsunterricht zu bestimmen.

(3) Der Religionsunterricht ist in den öffentlichen Schulen mit Ausnahme der bekenntnisfreien Schulen ordentliches Lehrfach. Unbeschadet des staatlichen Aufsichtsrechtes wird der Religionsunterricht in Übereinstimmung mit den Grundsätzen der Religionsgemeinschaften erteilt. Kein Lehrer darf gegen seinen Willen verpflichtet werden, Religionsunterricht zu erteilen.

(4) Das Recht zur Errichtung von privaten Schulen wird gewährleistet. Private Schulen als Ersatz für öffentliche Schulen bedürfen der Genehmigung des Staates und unterstehen den Landesgesetzen. Die Genehmigung ist zu erteilen, wenn die privaten Schulen in ihren Lehrzielen und Einrichtungen sowie in der wissenschaftlichen Ausbildung ihrer Lehrkräfte nicht hinter den öffentlichen Schulen zurückstehen und eine Sonderung der Schüler nach den Besitzverhältnissen der Eltern nicht gefördert wird. Die Genehmigung ist zu versagen, wenn die wirtschaftliche und rechtliche Stellung der Lehrkräfte nicht genügend gesichert ist.

(5) Eine private Volksschule ist nur zuzulassen, wenn die Unterrichtsverwaltung ein besonderes pädagogisches Interesse anerkennt oder, auf Antrag von Erziehungsberechtigten, wenn sie als Gemeinschaftsschule, als Bekenntnis- oder Weltan-

schauungsschule errichtet werden soll und eine öffentliche Volksschule dieser Art in der Gemeinde nicht besteht.

(6) Vorschulen bleiben aufgehoben.

Artikel 8

(1) Alle Deutschen haben das Recht, sich ohne Anmeldung oder Erlaubnis friedlich und ohne Waffen zu versammeln.

(2) Für Versammlungen unter freiem Himmel kann dieses Recht durch Gesetz oder auf Grund eines Gesetzes beschränkt werden.

Artikel 9

(1) Alle Deutschen haben das Recht, Vereine und Gesellschaften zu bilden.

(2) Vereinigungen, deren Zwecke oder deren Tätigkeit den Strafgesetzen zuwiderlaufen oder die sich gegen die verfassungsmäßige Ordnung oder gegen den Gedanken der Völkerverständigung richten, sind verboten.

(3) Das Recht, zur Wahrung und Förderung der Arbeits- und Wirtschaftsbedingungen Vereinigungen zu bilden, ist für jedermann und für alle Berufe gewährleistet. Abreden, die dieses Recht einschränken oder zu behindern suchen, sind nichtig, hierauf gerichtete Maßnahmen sind rechtswidrig.

Artikel 10

Das Briefgeheimnis sowie das Post- und Fernmeldegeheimnis sind unverletzlich. Beschränkungen dürfen nur auf Grund eines Gesetzes angeordnet werden.

Artikel 11

(1) Alle Deutschen genießen Freizügigkeit im ganzen Bundesgebiet.

(2) Dieses Recht darf nur durch Gesetz und nur für die Fälle eingeschränkt werden, in denen eine ausreichende Lebensgrundlage nicht vorhanden ist und der Allgemeinheit daraus besondere Lasten entstehen würden und in denen es zum Schutze der Jugend vor Verwahrlosung, zur Bekämpfung von Seuchengefahr oder um strafbaren Handlungen vorzubeugen, erforderlich ist.

Artikel 12[1])

(1) Alle Deutschen haben das Recht, Beruf, Arbeitsplatz und Ausbildungsstätte frei zu wählen. Die Berufsausübung kann durch Gesetz geregelt werden.

(2) Niemand darf zu einer bestimmten Arbeit gezwungen werden, außer im Rahmen einer herkömmlichen allgemeinen, für alle gleichen öffentlichen Dienstleistungspflicht. Wer aus Gewissensgründen den Kriegsdienst mit der Waffe verweigert, kann zu einem Ersatzdienst verpflichtet werden. Die Dauer des Ersatzdienstes darf die Dauer des Wehrdienstes nicht übersteigen. Das Nähere regelt ein Gesetz, das die Freiheit der Gewissensentscheidung nicht beeinträchtigen darf und auch eine Möglichkeit des Ersatzdienstes vorsehen muß, die in keinem Zusammenhang mit den Verbänden der Streitkräfte steht.

(3) Frauen dürfen nicht zu einer Dienstleistung im Verband der Streitkräfte durch Gesetz verpflichtet werden. Zu einem Dienst mit der Waffe dürfen sie in keinem Falle verwendet werden.

(4) Zwangsarbeit ist nur bei einer gerichtlich angeordneten Freiheitsentziehung zulässig.

Artikel 13

(1) Die Wohnung ist unverletzlich.

(2) Durchsuchungen dürfen nur durch den Richter, bei Gefahr im Verzuge auch durch die in den Gesetzen vorgesehenen anderen Organe angeordnet und nur in der dort vorgeschriebenen Form durchgeführt werden.

---

[1]) geändert durch Bundesgesetz vom 19. März 1956 (Bundesgesetzbl. I S. 111)

(3) Eingriffe und Beschränkungen dürfen im übrigen nur zur Abwehr einer gemeinen Gefahr oder einer Lebensgefahr für einzelne Personen, auf Grund eines Gesetzes auch zur Verhütung dringender Gefahren für die öffentliche Sicherheit und Ordnung, insbesondere zur Behebung der Raumnot, zur Bekämpfung von Seuchengefahr oder zum Schutze gefährdeter Jugendlicher vorgenommen werden.

Artikel 14

(1) Das Eigentum und das Erbrecht werden gewährleistet. Inhalt und Schranken werden durch die Gesetze bestimmt.

(2) Eigentum verpflichtet. Sein Gebrauch soll zugleich dem Wohle der Allgemeinheit dienen.

(3) Eine Enteignung ist nur zum Wohle der Allgemeinheit zulässig. Sie darf nur durch Gesetz oder auf Grund eines Gesetzes erfolgen, das Art und Ausmaß der Entschädigung regelt. Die Entschädigung ist unter gerechter Abwägung der Interessen der Allgemeinheit und der Beteiligten zu bestimmen. Wegen der Höhe der Entschädigung steht im Streitfalle der Rechtsweg vor den ordentlichen Gerichten offen.

Artikel 15

Grund und Boden, Naturschätze und Produktionsmittel können zum Zwecke der Vergesellschaftung durch ein Gesetz, das Art und Ausmaß der Entschädigung regelt, in Gemeineigentum oder in andere Formen der Gemeinwirtschaft übergeführt werden. Für die Entschädigung gilt Artikel 14 Absatz 3 Satz 3 und 4 entsprechend.

Artikel 16

(1) Die deutsche Staatsangehörigkeit darf nicht entzogen werden. Der Verlust der Staatsangehörigkeit darf nur auf Grund eines Gesetzes und gegen den Willen des Betroffenen nur dann eintreten, wenn der Betroffene dadurch nicht staatenlos wird.

(2) Kein Deutscher darf an das Ausland ausgeliefert werden. Politisch Verfolgte genießen Asylrecht.

Artikel 17

Jedermann hat das Recht, sich einzeln oder in Gemeinschaft mit anderen schriftlich mit Bitten oder Beschwerden an die zuständigen Stellen und an die Volksvertretung zu wenden.

Artikel 17a[1]

(1) Gesetze über Wehrdienst und Ersatzdienst können bestimmen, daß für die Angehörigen der Streitkräfte und des Ersatzdienstes während der Zeit des Wehr- oder Ersatzdienstes das Grundrecht, seine Meinung in Wort, Schrift und Bild frei zu äußern und zu verbreiten (Artikel 5 Absatz 1 Satz 1 erster Halbsatz), das Grundrecht der Versammlungsfreiheit (Artikel 8) und das Petitionsrecht (Artikel 17), soweit es das Recht gewährt, Bitten oder Beschwerden in Gemeinschaft mit anderen vorzubringen, eingeschränkt werden.

(2) Gesetze, die der Verteidigung einschließlich des Schutzes der Zivilbevölkerung dienen, können bestimmen, daß die Grundrechte der Freizügigkeit (Artikel 11) und der Unverletzlichkeit der Wohnung (Artikel 13) eingeschränkt werden.

Artikel 18

Wer die Freiheit der Meinungsäußerung, insbesondere die Pressefreiheit (Artikel 5 Absatz 1), die Lehrfreiheit (Artikel 5 Absatz 3), die Versammlungsfreiheit (Artikel 8), die Vereinigungsfreiheit (Artikel 9), das Brief-, Post- und Fernmeldegeheimnis (Artikel 10), das Eigentum (Artikel 14) oder das Asylrecht (Artikel 16 Absatz 2) zum Kampfe gegen die freiheitliche demokratische Grundordnung mißbraucht, verwirkt diese Grundrechte. Die Verwirkung und ihr Ausmaß werden durch das Bundesverfassungsgericht ausgesprochen.

---

[1]) eingefügt durch Bundesgesetz vom 19. März 1956 (Bundesgesetzbl. I S. 111)

Artikel 19

(1) Soweit nach diesem Grundgesetz ein Grundrecht durch Gesetz oder auf Grund eines Gesetzes eingeschränkt werden kann, muß das Gesetz allgemein und nicht nur für den Einzelfall gelten. Außerdem muß das Gesetz das Grundrecht unter Angabe des Artikels nennen.

(2) In keinem Falle darf ein Grundrecht in seinem Wesensgehalt angetastet werden.

(3) Die Grundrechte gelten auch für inländische juristische Personen, soweit sie ihrem Wesen nach auf diese anwendbar sind.

(4) Wird jemand durch die öffentliche Gewalt in seinen Rechten verletzt, so steht ihm der Rechtsweg offen. Soweit eine andere Zuständigkeit nicht begründet ist, ist der ordentliche Rechtsweg gegeben.

587. UNIVERSAL DECLARATION OF HUMAN RIGHTS
December 10, 1948

(U. N. General Assembly, 2d. Session, Doc. A/811)

This Universal Declaration of Human Rights, drafted by a U. N. Commission on Human Rights headed by Eleanor Roosevelt, was agreed upon by the 1948 General Assembly, with only the Russian bloc opposed. As no provision was made for its enforcement, the Declaration has served largely as a statement of moral principles. See Z. Chafee, *Documents on Fundamental Human Rights;* A. N. Holcombe, *Human Rights in the Modern World;* R. N. Baldwin, *Human Rights, World Declaration and American Practice.*

THE GENERAL ASSEMBLY

Proclaims this Universal Declaration of Human Rights as a common standard of achievement for all peoples and all nations to the end that every individual and every organ of society, keeping this declaration constantly in mind, shall strive by teaching and education to promote respect for these rights and freedoms and by progressive measures, national and international, to secure their universal and effective recognition and observance, both among the peoples of Member States themselves and among the peoples of territories under their jurisdiction.

Art. 1. All human beings are born free and equal in dignity and rights. They are endowed with reason and conscience and should act towards one another in a spirit of brotherhood.

Art. 2. Everyone is entitled to all the rights and freedoms set forth in this Declaration, without distinction of any kind, such as race, colour, sex, language, religion, political or other opinion, national or social origin, property, birth, or other status.

Furthermore, no distinction shall be made on the basis of the political, jurisdictional, or international status of the country or territory to which a person belongs, whether it be an independent, trust, or non-self-governing territory or under any limitation of sovereignty.

Art. 3. Everyone has the right to life, liberty, and security of person.

Art. 4. No one shall be held in slavery or servitude; slavery and the slave trade shall be prohibited in all their forms.

Art. 5. No one shall be subjected to torture or to cruel, inhuman, or degrading treatment or punishment.

Art. 6. Everyone has the right to recognition everywhere as a person before the law.

Art. 7. All are equal before the law and are entitled without any discrimination to equal protection of the law. All are entitled to equal protection against any discrimination in violation of this Declaration and against any incitement to such discrimination.

Art. 8. Everyone has the right to an effective remedy by the competent national tribunals for acts violating the fundamental rights granted him by the Constitution or by law.

Art. 9. No one shall be subjected to arbitrary arrest, detention, or exile.

Art. 10. Everyone is entitled in full equality to a fair and public hearing by an independent and impartial tribunal, in the determination of his rights and obligations and of any criminal charge against him.

Art. 11. 1. Everyone charged with a penal offence has the right to be presumed innocent until proved guilty according to law in a public trial at which he has had all the guarantees necessary for his defence.

2. No one shall be held guilty of any penal offence on account of any act or omission which did not constitute a penal offence, under national or international law, at the time when it was committed. Nor shall a heavier penalty be imposed than the one that was applicable at the time the penal offence was committed.

Art. 12. No one shall be subjected to arbitrary interference with his privacy, family, home, or correspondence, nor to attacks upon his honour and reputation. Everyone has the right to the protection of the law against such interference or attacks.

Art. 13. 1. Everyone has the right to freedom of movement and residence within the borders of each State.

2. Everyone has the right to leave any country, including his own, and to return to his country.

Art. 14. 1. Everyone has the right to seek and to enjoy in other countries asylum from persecution.

2. This right may not be invoked in the case of prosecutions genuinely arising from non-political crimes or from acts contrary to the purposes and principles of the United Nations.

Art 15. 1. Everyone has the right to a nationality.

2. No one shall be arbitrarily deprived of his nationality nor denied the right to change his nationality.

Art. 16. 1. Men and women of full age, without any limitation due to race, nationality, or religion, have the right to marry and to found a family. They are entitled to equal rights as to marriage, during marriage, and at its disolution.

2. Marriage shall be entered into only with the free and full consent of the intending spouses.

3. The family is the natural and fundamental group unit of society and is entitled to protection by society and the State.

Art. 17. 1. Everyone has the right to own property alone as well as in association with others.

2. No one shall be arbitrarily deprived of his property.

Art. 18. Everyone has the right to freedom of thought, conscience, and religion; this right includes freedom to change his religion or belief, and freedom either alone or in community with others and in public or private, to manifest his religion or belief in teaching, practice, worship, and observance.

Art. 19. Everyone has the right to freedom of opinion and expression, this right includes freedom to hold opinions without interference and to seek, receive, and impart information and ideas through any media and regardless of frontiers.

Art. 20. 1. Everyone has the right to freedom of peaceful assembly and association.

2. No one may be compelled to belong to an association.

Art. 21. 1. Everyone has the right to take part in the Government of his country, directly or through freely chosen representatives.

2. Everyone has the right of equal access to public service in his country.

3. The will of the people shall be the basis of the authority of Government; this will shall be expressed in periodic and genuine elections which shall be by universal and equal suffrage and shall be held by secret vote or by equivalent free voting procedures.

Art. 22. Everyone as a member of society, has the right to social security and is entitled to the realisation, through national effort and international co-operation and in accordance with the organisation and resources of each State, of the economic, social, and cultural rights indispensable for his dignity and the free development of his personality.

Art. 23. 1. Everyone has the right to work, to free choice of employment, to just and favourable conditions of work, and to protection aaginst unemployment.

2. Everyone, without any discrimination, has the right to equal pay for equal work.

3. Everyone who works has the right to just and favourable remuneration, insuring for himself and his family an existence worthy of human dignity, and supplemented, if necessary by other means of social protection.

4. Everyone has the right to form and to join trade unions for the protection of his

interests.

Art. 24. Everyone has the right to rest and leisure, including reasonable limitation of working hours and periodic holidays with pay.

Art. 25. 1. Everyone has the right to a standard of living adequate for the health and wellbeing of himself and of his family, including food, clothing, housing, and medical care and necessary social services, and the right to security in the event of unemployment, sickness disability, widowhood, old age, or other lack of livelihood in circumstances beyond his control.

2. Motherhood and childhood are entitled to special care and assistance. All children, whether born in or out of wedlock, shall enjoy the same social protection.

Art. 26. 1. Everyone has the right to education. Education shall be free, at least in the elementary and fundamental stages. Elementary education shall be compulsory. Technical and professional education shall be made generally available, and higher education shall be equally accessible to all on the basis of merit.

2. Education shall be directed to the full development of the human personality and to the strengthening of respect for human rights and fundamental freedoms, it shall promote understanding, tolerance, and friendship among all nations, racial or religious groups, and shall further the activities of the United Nations for the maintenance of peace.

3. Parents have a prior right to choose the kind of education that shall be given to their children.

Art. 27. 1. Everyone has the right freely to participate in the cultural life of the community, to enjoy the arts, and to share in scientific advancement and its benefits.

2. Everyone has the right to the protection of the moral and material interests resulting from any scientific, literary, or artistic production of which he is the author.

Art. 28. Everyone is entitled to a social and international order in which the rights and freedoms set forth in this declaration can be fully realised.

Art. 29. 1. Everyone has duties to the community in which alone the free and full development of his personality is possible.

2. In the exercise of his rights and freedoms, everyone shall be subject only to such limitations as are determined by law solely for the purpose of securing due recognition and respect for the rights and freedoms of others and of meeting the just requirements of morality, public order, and the general welfare in a democratic society.

3. These rights and freedoms may in no case be exercised contrary to the purposes and principles of the United Nations.

Art. 30. Nothing in this Declaration may be interpreted as implying for any State, group, or person any right to engage in any activity or to perform any act aimed at the destruction of any of the rights and freedoms set forth herein.

Acknowlegements

We are grateful to the following for permission to reprint these texts:

Additional text page 21:
Edward L. Schapsmeier and Frederick H. Schapsmeier, Political Parties and Civic Action Groups, Greenwood, Press Inc., Westport, CT USA, 1981. Copyright © 1981 by Edward L. Schapsmeier and Frederick H. Schapsmeier. Reprinted with permission.

Page 45:
Excerpts from the Journals of Sylvia Plath, edited by Ted Hughes and Frances McCullough, Copyright © 1982 by Ted Hughes. Reprinted by permission of Doubleday, a division of Bantam, Doubleday, Dell Publishing Group, Inc.

Page 50:
From an article in the Washington Post, October 3, 1970 by Renee Ferguson "Women's Liberation Has Different Meaning for Blacks". Reprinted by Permission of the Washington Post.

Page 97:
Rights controlled by Harriet Wassermann Literary Agency, Inc., New York